THE PRO KNOW-HOW™ BOOK OF

Logo Design Theory

How Branding Design Really Works

Edition 2.1

A. Michael Shumate

Logo Design Theory:
How Branding Design Really Works
by A. Michael Shumate

ISBN: 978-1-7770168-0-7

© 2021 by A. Michael Shumate

Published by Elfstone Press
PO Box 64
Cardigan, PE
Canada C0A 1G0
elfstonepress.com

Cover: Identities used on the cover, on title page and on Chapter pages were designed by the author.

All illustrations (except those featuring other people's logos, images otherwise noted and photographs) are Copyright by A. Michael Shumate. Some are available for stock use through Gettyone.com; others are available directly through the author or Elfstone Press.

Note on Edition 2.1
This edition has fifteen new or amended images as well as several additions or clarifications in the text.

As a courtesy, names of all designers whose work is shown as a negative or indifferent examples are not shown.

Every effort has been made to give credit for all identities shown as good examples. Even so, any designer whose work is shown herein may request credit shown for said work by contacting (editorail@elfstonepress.com) and credit will be shown in the next printing of this book. Feedback is also actively sought on other corrections or new examples of principles outlined in this book.

PRO KNOW HOW BOOKS™

Pro Know-How™ Books are not written for dummies or for complete idiots. Instead, they are written by experienced professionals for people who aspire to acquire skills at a professional level through study and applied effort.

Table of Contents

Introduction

The first day of teaching new college students, I tell them to call me Michael, not Professor Shumate or Mr. Shumate. Then I tell them that if they forget my name, they can always call me Grand Poobah. The term comes from the Gilbert and Sullivan musical *The Mikado* and is one of many titles that an officious character has bestowed upon himself. The term Grand Poobah has come to mean "anyone with no real authority but who acts otherwise" (as defined, appropriately enough, in Wikipedia).

There you have it. I will speak with great authority where I have none, except that which experience has given me.

And what is my experience? I graduated with a BFA degree in Graphic Design, and I've been a professional designer and illustrator for over fifty years. My work has been used all over the world by many major companies. I have worked in virtually every area of graphic design: identity design, advertising, institutional, signage and interpretive display design. I have created identities in all areas of branding: commercial, government, institutional, product and retail. In addition to freelancing, I was a Professor of Graphic Design and Illustration at St. Lawrence College in Ontario, where I taught for twenty-five years. I am now Professor Emeritus.

There are some who say, "Those who can, do, and those who can't, teach." That may apply to some teachers. (Judge for yourself; see my branding portfolio at the end of this book.) But there is also another old saying, "The teacher learns more than the students."

In my career, I have created dozens of corporate identity designs, but in my teaching I have guided students to create thousands of identity designs. It is that kind of design perspective I wish to share.

When grading student work I had an obligation to evaluate the work and give concrete reasons for the grades assigned. I found that it was not good enough to point out failings; I had to try to teach how to avoid those failings in the first place.

I won't quote other design books to justify my positions; I'll just show each principle or issue and let your own eyes bear witness to you what is or isn't true. You will see for yourself what works and what doesn't.

As a teacher, I always looked for a book I could adopt for my courses that would summarize sound principles of logo design. I never found one. Instead, this is the book that I wished my students could have studied.

Over 25 years, the exercise of grading student work against standards that are solid and enduring has given me insights into the principles of branding design that I have not seen shared anywhere else. I wish to pass them on.

This will be a personal book, from me to you, a fellow designer. My hope is to save you years of trial and error and speed you on to succeed in your corporate identity design endeavors. Perhaps you will look at this art of branding design with new eyes and be a little wiser and directed in your work.

I wish you success.

A. Michael Shumate
BFA, RGD Emeritus
Professor Emeritus St. Lawrence College
a.k.a. Grand Poobah

Foundational Principles of Graphic Design

In our digital age many design schools
concentrate so much on software
that some basic precepts may be missing from the curriculum.
Here are some essential principles
that have a huge impact on branding design.

Chapter 1

Professional, Prima Donna or Artsy-Fartsy?

Prima donna was originally a term for the principal woman soloist in an opera production, and literally means the "first lady." The term is also used to describe a self-important person who may be capable artistically, but is also insufferably demanding and difficult to please. Now if we call someone a prima donna, it is an insult. It implies a person who is rude, proud, self-centered and opportunistic—a talented brat.

While we can see that artistic achievers are sometimes afflicted with these negative human traits, we ought not swallow the lie that their creative achievement came *because* of those traits. It came *in spite* of them.

In contrast, a professional has both pride and humility. Here is a simple definition of a professional: a person who can do a good job and who works in good faith for the benefit of his or her client. A professional puts the client above self. He or she takes appropriate pride in putting the job first and in being capable of consistent excellence. The humility is recognition that the performer is not the center of attention. The performance is.

"Mr. Self-Important" by A. Michael Shumate, 1990

If I go to see my dentist and he says, "How about a root canal today? You don't really need one, but I love to do them," I would consider him to be terribly unprofessional. I would never return and would do what I could to see that he didn't ever practice dentistry again.

If I consulted a lawyer about a simple matter, and he suggested that we launch a lawsuit, when much more direct or less costly methods had not been explored, I might feel the same.

Any professional I hire is supposed to act in *my* best interests.

Artsy-fartsies are so enamored of the experience of doing something they enjoy that they do not see or care if what they want is in the best interest of the client. This tendency is not confined to artistic professions as we saw in the examples of the lawyer and dentist just mentioned.

Designers, being in an artistic occupation, often have to prove they are not artsy-fartsy flakes, but rather, can be a valued part of a whole business team. We can and should be key players that bring specialized expertise and prove that good design benefits a business.

And so it is in corporate-identity design: a professional branding designer is one who creates identities in the best interest of the client, not one who does what feels most "creative" or what might get recognition from peers. A professionally designed identity is one that will work well for the client in *all* situations, not in just some formats.

As this book unfolds, I hope that I will be able to explain each design principle clearly enough that we will agree, in the end, that there are solid principles of identity design that we can adopt to become, in every sense of the word, professional designers.

Chapter 2

Seeking True Principles in Art and Design

"Birth of the Virgin,"
by Pietro Lorenzettti , 1342

"The Delivery of the Keys" (detail), 1481–1482. Pietro Perugino was among the first artists to adopt Brunelleschi's principles of linear perspective, which allowed an artist to not only draw architecture accurately but correctly calculate the sizes of people in a three dimensional space.

Discovering Perspective

Before the Renaissance, artists knew that parallel lines in architecture appeared to taper at different angles, but their attempts to show this realistically in painting were inconsistent at best. This resulted in lots of paintings with wonky architecture.

It wasn't until about 1425, that Filippo Brunelleschi figured out the underlying principles of linear perspective. All across Europe there was a smacking sound as artists slapped their foreheads and said, "Mama mia! Of course!" Once the secret was disclosed, everyone could see it clearly and virtually all artists quickly adopted this principle. Why?

Because it worked.

Unravelling Color Secrets

In the mid 1800s a chemist named Eugene Chevreul was the dye-master for the Gobelins Tapestry Works in Paris. He did extensive experiments combining threads of different colors. He formulated the theory of simultaneous contrast of colors after observing that threads of very different hue look richer when next to each other. Many of the impressionists and post-impressionists were thrilled with the practical application of Chevreul's principles.

Vincent van Gogh even kept different colored balls of yarn to work out specific color combinations. His paintings, more than any other of those painters, resembled separate threads of color. And what beauty van Gogh created with the principles Chevreul discovered.

"Olive Trees," 1854. Van Gogh and other impressionists and post-impressionists reveled in what they could do using Chevreul's color principles of simultaneous contrast.

Ephemeral or Eternal?

In my second week of teaching college Branding Design, I told a student that the logo concept he was working on would not be suitable as a professional identity design. He asked me, "Why?"

I answered that I didn't know why, but that his concept was still a bad idea. I was certain some principle was being violated, but I couldn't articulate what it was. I also knew that my answer was totally inadequate. I determined then and there that I would discover what those underlying principles were and teach them.

That twenty-five year quest has lead me to look deeply at branding design and to seek for those constant, unchanging principles. Fads in art and design come and go. But principles don't. Principles are enduring; they stand the test of time. We can ignore them for a while, but violating principles just breaks our work. Over time, we come back to true principles. Why?

Because they work. They always work.

I believe there are true principles in every area of artistic endeavor including branding design. I don't pretend to know them all, but I'm sure I've discovered at least a few. Those are what I want to share here in this book.

It doesn't matter where knowledge comes from; when we find true principles, we would do well to pay attention and adopt them.

Bedrock principles in graphic design trump fad and fashion every time. There are few areas where this is more evident than in branding design. Designers whose identities violate those principles will find that, sooner or later, their creations will be replaced.

Those who vainly seek to be on the leading edge find out, more often than not, that they are on the bleeding edge. The underlying principles of identity design don't change. Those who cater to temporary swings in taste will find their work goes out of style quickly. Sadly, designers who think that they can do anything and call it an identity don't understand the nature of corporate identity at all.

Chapter 3

Four Myths About Creativity

"Creativity" by A. Michael Shumate, 1990

Much has been written and spoken about creativity. A lot of it is dry, academic stuff, using big words and obscure concepts to describe this most intriguing thing called creativity. There's also a fair bit of folk legend on the subject. Some of those ideas on creativity are as fanciful as frog feathers. I'm not claiming that frog feathers aren't real, maybe they are. All I know is that all frogs of my acquaintance have no feathers. Likewise, many of these notions about creativity are quite different from my experiences.

Let's look at this subject anyway.

What Creativity Isn't

Sometimes it helps to define something by eliminating things that are confused with it. That exercise will be particularly useful in our discussion of creativity. Let's dispel some myths.

MYTH #1: CREATIVITY IS DOING WHATEVER COMES INTO YOUR HEAD. While it is true that there are brainstorming techniques that do just that–elicit anything that pops into the participants' minds–this is not the basis of true creativity. We'll come back to brainstorming later.

MYTH #2: CREATIVITY IS DOING WHATEVER YOU WANT. We live in a culture of elitism that reenforces this myth. It originated

"School of Athens" by Raphael, 1511

in Renaissance times. It became an accepted practice then to give special license to supposedly creative people. It was a concept of celebrity status that considers these artistic folks were somehow above the average person and above the normal rules of conduct.

Michelangelo was certainly one of the greatest artists of the Renaissance. Unfortunately, he really bought into this notion of artistic entitlement and milked it for all he was worth. A very talented artist contemporary of Michelangelo's, named Raphael, used to poke fun at him for his anti-social ways. Raphael even painted a large fresco for the Pope titled "The School of Athens," which includes two persons representing Plato and Aristotle. The face of Plato is a portrait of Leonardo da Vinci, who Raphael honored. Other great philosophers and artists have the faces of other contemporaries that

Raphael admired. He even painted himself (looking out) with a few of his artist friends in a little group at the right side of the scene. Front and center in this fresco he put Michelangelo, sitting on a step and sulking. Raphael, who was an excellent artist himself, had very little patience with Michelangelo putting on "artsy-fartsy" airs.

Sadly, we still uphold the same artists-are-different delusion today. It's a notion fostered by self-indulgent persons who want license to act badly. Unfortunately, it is well ingrained in our society, but it ought not to be. Creativity is no license to be self-centered, selfish or rude, any more than being wealthy or famous should give folks license to be boorish.

MYTH #3: CREATIVITY JUST HAPPENS WHEN YOU ARE INSPIRED. The ancient Greeks believed that there were goddesses, called the Muses, who gave artists inspiration. The word inspire

means to "breathe in" or "inhale," and the word inspiration originally meant to be "breathed upon" by the gods.

Many people today may not believe in literal muses, but they still insist that creativity involves waiting for "inspiration" to light upon our shoulders and give us ideas. The notion that the truly creative individual can only create when "in the mood" is both undisciplined and untrue and is the battle-cry of the lazy and under-achievers. The real creative geniuses of our world worked at their art, whether they were in the mood or not. Thomas Edison said, "Genius is one percent inspiration, ninety-nine percent perspiration."

MYTH #4: CREATIVITY IS JUST BREAKING THE BOUNDARIES. That is the shallowest myth of all. Just breaking boundaries serves little purpose in and of itself, unless it solves a problem. To be sure, many a creative solution requires a new approach, but a new and different approach, just for its own sake, doesn't constitute a creative one.

What Creativity Is

In the final analysis, creativity is the ability to solve problems.

There. That was easy. That's really what it's all about.

When you have a problem there are always constraints, limitations and boundaries that come as part of the problem. An important aspect of creativity is having clear vision to correctly perceive a problem and the constraints around it. That vision will also see real limitations as separate and different from imagined limitations.

Let's say you've got a glass jar with a metal lid that you can't open. You could smash the jar to separate the lid from the jar. That's new and different, but that's hardly a creative solution. Nor is it a suitable solution. One of the real constraints of this problem is that, most of the time, the jar needs to remain intact after it's open or its contents will be ruined if mixed with broken glass.

A creative solution might be that you pry a bit all around the edges of the lid to break the seal. You could run some hot water over the lid, but not the jar, to get the metal lid to expand a bit more than the jar and loosen up. You could wrap rubber bands around the lid and around the jar to increase the traction of your grip.

Some people think that a solution must be new and different in order to be creative. How superficial. Being new and different is not the necessary ingredient. Solving the problem is what is necessary.

If you stop and think about it, "new and different" has already been done.

So don't worry about it.

"The Unmaze" by A. Michael Shumate, 1989

8

Chapter 4

What is the Purpose of Graphic Design?

I was once in an elevator with the custodian of our building. I knew him by name, and he knew I was a professor of graphic design. This day he proudly announced to me that he planned to open his own graphic design business.

"Really?" I responded with genuine curiosity. This man had never mentioned graphic design before.

"Yes. I just got a new computer and now *I can choose fonts*."

I was dumbfounded. It was apparent that he thought that choosing fonts was all there was to graphic design. To reinforce his position, he continued, "I designed my first brochure last night, and I used twenty-eight different fonts!"

Mercifully, the elevator door opened on my floor and I got out.

This kind of idea is all too common, even among graphic design students and a few novice practitioners. They feel a graphic designer's job is to "jazz-up" the content, "make it look cool" or "make it fancy." While jazzing-up a design may be appropriate in some circumstances, it might be disastrous in others, and it is *not* the underlying purpose of good graphic design.

So, just what is the real purpose of graphic design?

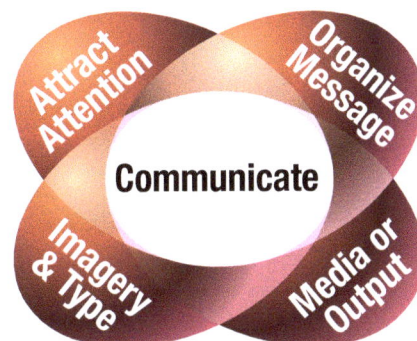

To aid communication.

This can be accomplished in several ways:

1. ATTRACTING ATTENTION. In our world of never-ending messages, one must first get a pair of eyes to look at a message before it can be communicated. Designers use tools like typography, layout, color and imagery to do this. So esthetics do matter.

2. ORGANIZING THE MESSAGE. Complex messages or bodies of information must be broken down into manageable and logical subsets, as well as a logical order. This is essential in media such as brochures and web sites.

3. USING IMAGERY & TYPE CORRECTLY. A given design can lead with imagery or with type. Type can be a kind of imagery in itself. When used together, there needs to be a hierarchy in the elements to control the viewer's eyes and the communication experience.

4. USING THE RIGHT MEDIA OR OUTPUT AND USING THE MEDIA CORRECTLY. This may seem too obvious to mention, but the physical form of the media can give advantages but also imposes limitations. A poster does not work like a website. A brochure has different parameters compared to a business card. Signage is not the same as a magazine ad.

A successful corporate identity design needs to work effectively in each of those situations.

All of these considerations should not distract us from this principle: the primary job of graphic design is *to facilitate communication.* Anything that compromises that core function of communication is counter-productive.

9

Chapter 5

Form Follows Function

A few years ago I shopped for a tool to help me get rid of dandelions in my lawn. I have an aversion to herbicides, and snipping the tops of the plants does little. The roots, which are several inches deep, must come out. I came home with a dandelion digger that looked both sturdy and elegant, ostensibly a good design from a respected brand. But when I went to use it, I found the job harder than I had expected, and it left gaping two-inch holes in my lawn.

The next day, I exchanged the tool for one that wasn't as expensive or attractive, but was easier to use and left much smaller holes—more like ones you get when you aerate your lawn. Since the primary function of the tool was not appearance or fashion, I was fine with the way it looked. How it worked was the most important consideration.

One of the most ubiquitous maxims in art and craft is "Form Follows Function." And it contains a great deal of truth.

If a form impedes function or creates new problems, it is a poor design. While it is not wrong to re-evaluate the specific function we might be seeking, the form we choose had better not impede that core function.

It is sometimes easy to get distracted from the essential function of a creative project. This is especially true when esthetics are an integral part of the function as with corporate identity. But esthetics are not the only function of a corporate identity. Clear thinking must override gut impulses in this area.

What is the function of a corporate identity?

Here again it is important to get our vision straight. The functions of any corporate identity are:

1. To be seen and recognized instantly,

2. To appropriately and positively represent the business/organization/product being identified,

3. To be consistently reproducible and maintain clarity across all media,

4. To be flexible enough to be used in a wide variety of design and media environments.

If we create a design that fails in any of these four functions, we have failed to create a workable design. Period.

Some people know how to make solid, useful identities. For many others, the process is hit-or-miss. Some designers seem fixated on doing something that has never been done before, not only in their specific design, but in their very approach. Perhaps they believe that because they produced something new, they have been terribly creative. What they may forget to do is test their finished identity design against the four functions above. If it doesn't pass *all* four of those tests, such a creation shouldn't even be presented to the client.

Maybe the reason why people never used that approach before, is that it *doesn't work*.

Remember that in the end, creativity is the ability to find the best way to solve a problem. Period.

Creativity is often characterized as a new way of doing something. That is because a new problem sometimes requires a new solution. That's why we notice it. But the core of creativity is not that it is new. That's a common fallacy of logic called Association with Causation—a false notion that because two events occur together, one causes the other. Corn and pumpkins often ripen at the same time, but the corn does not make the pumpkins ripen, or vice versa.

For any problem, there may be many new and different approaches that will NOT provide a solution. Theoretically only a few, or perhaps even only one approach will succeed.

Λ problem does not always reside outside of the status quo. It may touch that circle tangentally. This can mean that the most suitable solution will not require anything new to solve it. This is a common irritant to those who desperately aspire to their notion that "creativity means being new and different" at all costs. They insist that newness is an essential part of any solution. This fixation is almost epidemic in creative fields like graphic design. The tragic flaw is that the new and unusual approach may fail to solve the problem at hand.

Sad to say, many design annuals abound in examples of "bleeding edge" design—the cutting edge that has gone too far and doesn't work. Where the form does not follow the function.

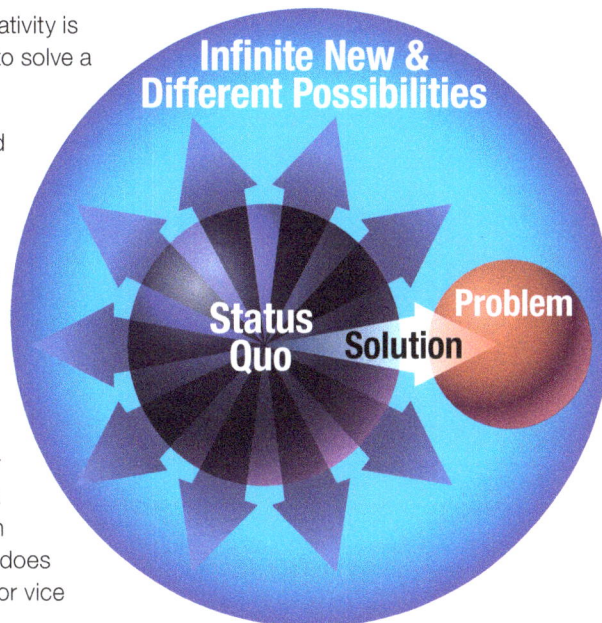

And if a design doesn't function in the client's best interests, it isn't professional (even if the designer gets paid for it). Sooner or later the client may recognize that the design just doesn't work and go elsewhere for a new design that does work. This happens all too often in the field of identity design.

Designing identities that work in all situations is eminently doable—*if* you know the principles of good design, which we're about to get to.

Infinite New & Different Possibilities

Status Quo

Solution

Problem

Chapter 6

Basic Principles of Design

We live in a graphic savvy culture. Design infuses everything from the gadgets we use to communicate and play, to the clothes we wear, to the bottle our shampoo comes in. Every brochure we pick up, every ad in a magazine, every commercial on TV is designed. It is said that the average person now is exposed to more than 3,000 images a day. We are almost force-fed images all day, every day.

But just because we eat every day doesn't mean we know how to cook.

Adobe Creative Cloud apps (Photoshop, Illustrator, InDesign, etc.) have been downloaded an astounding 237 million times (as of 2018). In addition, there is other graphics-capable software in use today.

Many users have no design training.

Even those with formal training don't necessarily know what they're doing. Many schools now focus curriculum more on software and less on design principles. People who know only the programs, not design, are sometimes hired to teach new generations of graphic designers. The result? Graphic design graduates with a lack of good grounding in their field.

Because of this, bad design abounds.

Just because we **EAT** every day doesn't mean we know how to **COOK**

In opposition to the tide of design illiteracy, let's agree on four basic principles of design.

Principle #1:
Simplicity is the Soul of Good Design

Beginning designers often get to a stage in a project where they sense that the design is not working and ask themselves, "What else does this need?"

More often they should be asking, "What do I need to delete?" This is especially true with corporate identity design. The best identities are simple and are the more memorable and effective for it.

Simplicity
is the
SOUL
of good
Design

"Plugged In" by A. Michael Shumate, 1992

Principle #2:
Computers Don't Design for You

Even if we could plug computers directly into our brains, it would still be necessary to know what our end product *should* look like before we could design it.

At the beginning of my career, I usually made my master logos with pen and ink. Now, I always design identities with a vector computer program. It is the tool of choice in our industry. These programs offer capabilities that cannot be duplicated by hand, but they still need our know-how to work. Computers don't design on their own, in the esthetic sense. Generally speaking, computers don't do what we *want* them to do. They do what we *tell* them to do. It's up to us to know which shapes, sizes, relationships and colors will work. I call this Visual Knowledge. If we don't have that Visual Knowledge, the computer can't supply it. Computers supply mathematically-based processes, not visual knowledge.

A computer won't tell you if your shapes are esthetically mismatched. A computer can tell you what size your elements are, but it doesn't know if those sizes are appropriate together. That's your job.

In the end, if you can't draw, you can't draw on the computer. If you can't design, you can't design on the computer.

Early in my teaching career, I taught a course called Graphic Techniques. It covered many difficult esthetic and manual skills that graphic designers used to need. One of my students was on the brink of failing. He begged me to let him have the benefit of the doubt. "I'm a whiz on the computer," he said. "You'll see."

He barely passed that course, and when we got to the computer-based design, his work was horrible. His designs were all techno-crap.

The lesson: computers don't supply esthetics.

Principle #3: Beware BYC Design

When I began graphic design, we didn't use computers. If we wanted a gradient in a design, there were two ways to get it.

1. We hired an airbrush artist to paint the gradient, then had it photographed, photo-separated and spliced into plate negatives by a photoengraver.

2. We could have the photoengravers (if they knew how) make the gradients directly. Either way, some of the control was relinquished to the airbrush artists and photoengravers.

In both cases gradients were so expensive, they were seldom worth squandering the design budget on. Nowadays there are very few airbrush artists (good thing, too; with all the heavy-metal pigments in the air, this was a hazardous profession). Today most airbrushing is done in Photoshop. Also, the whole profession of photoengraving has almost vanished. Our designs go from the computer directly to plates without anyone having to make color separations (which used to be expensive in their own right) or stripping together and registering the separate negatives from which to burn the printing plates.

Some of those processes that used to be so expensive are easy to do now; the only thing they cost today's designers is the trouble of clicking a certain button. That has created an epidemic of BYC Design.

What does it mean? "Because You Can." That is an extremely shallow reason for doing something. Sadly, when it's the designer's *only* reason, the design usually suffers.

Principle #4: Beware JTBD Design

Only slightly better than BYC design is JTBD Design, "Just to Be Different."

Not that novelty is a bad thing. It's great *if* it doesn't cause other problems like bad legibility, poor reproduction, or greater costs for the client (remember, not acting in the client's best interest is inherently unprofessional). Measured against the possible downsides, novelty alone can be a poor bargain.

Next we'll get to some design principles you can really buy into.

(Given the moral of this story, this kitschy type treatment is ironically appropriate.)

Chapter 7

Legibility and Contrast

Basic Terms

Before we launch into a discussion of color and contrast, let's make sure we are using the same language. Three terms may be used in describing any given color.

First is **HUE**, how colors distinguish themselves from each other in the rainbow or in the spectrum. Yellow is different from orange and from red, etc. It is also how colors are differentiated around a color wheel.

Second is **SATURATION**, the relative richness or dullness of a color. All colors in the spectrum are fully saturated (except at the ends, where they lapse into black). Dusty rose is less saturated (or more neutral) than pink. Olive is a less saturated version of yellow-green.

The third term is **VALUE**, which is the inherent lightness or darkness of a color. Going around a properly constructed color wheel, the lightest color is yellow and the darkest is blue.

Of the more than two million colors that a normal human eye can discern, each one can be described using these three terms, the way we could use three axis points to determine the position of something in three-dimensional space or the size of something using height, width and depth.

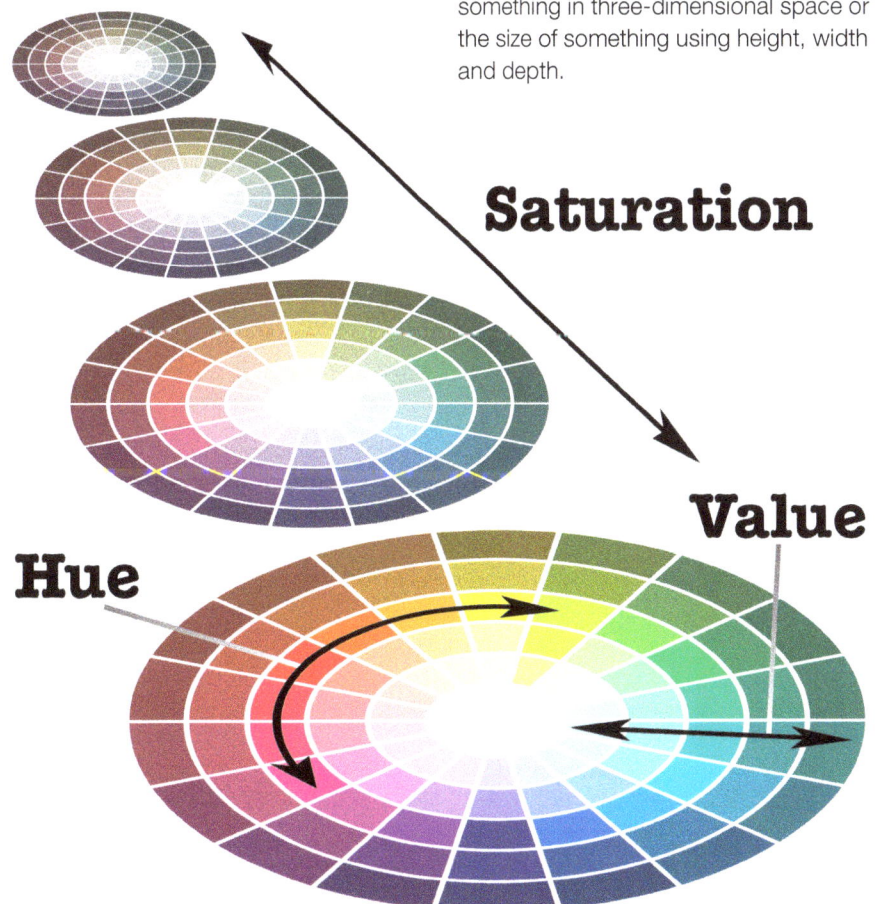

Saturation

Value

Hue

Legibility

When we can see and read what is written or perceive the elements of a picture, we call that legibility. Legibility is a function of contrast.

Legibility is a function of contrast
Legibility is a function of contrast
Legibility is a function of contrast
Legibility is a function of contrast
Legibility is a function of contrast
Legibility is a function of contrast
Legibility is a function of contrast
Legibility is a function of contrast
Legibility is a function of contrast
Legibility is a function of contrast
Legibility is a function of contrast

Of the three qualities of color we just defined—hue, saturation and value—the one that matters most for contrast is value. Saturation and hue hardly make a difference, especially when distance or small size is involved.

To sum up so far: legibility is a function of contrast, and contrast is a function of value.

legibility is a function of contrast, and contrast is a function of value.

In graphic design, nothing compensates for a lack of legibility. No concept. No style or fashion. No coolness factor. I repeat: Nothing compensates for a lack of legibility. Without it, no one even sees or correctly perceives your work. This is fundamental.

A good tool for accurately describing values is tint percentage, developed in the printing industry. Halftone tints cover an area with a small uniform grid of dots on a paper, often smaller than can be seen with the naked eye. In a 70% halftone tint, 70% of the paper area is covered in ink and only 30% of the paper has no ink. These halftone tint percentages should be second nature to all graphic designers.

Surprint 10%	20%	30%	40%	50%
	20%	30%	40%	50%
	90%	80%	70%	60%
100% Reverse	90%	80%	70%	60%

Halftone tint percentages are a convenient way to describe value in concrete terms.

Contrast Differential

The amount of contrast between type and its background can be calculated by subtracting the lesser value percentage from the greater. This is the Contrast Differential. A good rule of thumb for excellent contrast is 60% difference or more. Black type on white paper is a 100% difference, the greatest contrast possible, whereas 35% contrast differential is minimal.

Is it physically possible to read below that threshold? Yes, of course. But is it convenient or comfortable? No. And what is the function of graphic design? To *aid* communication, not impede it. Why would any sane designer try to make the printed message anything less than convenient or comfortable to read?

There is no good reason.

100% over 80% = 20% difference:	Insufficient
45% over 80% = 35% difference:	Marginal
30% over 80% = 50% difference:	Adequate
20% over 80% = 60% difference:	Excellent
100% over 60% = 40% difference:	Marginal
40% over 60% = 20% difference:	Insufficient
25% over 60% = 35% difference:	Marginal
0% over 60% = 60% difference:	Excellent
100% over 30% = 70% difference:	Excellent
65% over 30% = 35% difference:	Marginal
50% over 30% = 20% difference:	Insufficient
10% over 30% = 20% difference:	Insufficient

Viewing this from a distance of even a few feet shows the need for excellent contrast.

**When to Reverse and
When to Surprint**

If one accepts the logic of the foregoing, one would naturally think that a designer would be safe to place black type on a background as dark as 40% or 50%.

The reality is that such type is tiresome, even oppressive, to read.

Why is that?

0%	10%	20%	30%	40%	50%	60%	70%	80%	90%	100%

White White White White White White White White
White White White White White White White White

10% 10% 10% 10% 10% 10% 10% 10% 10%
10% 10% 10% 10% 10% 10% 10% 10% 10%

20% 20% 20% 20% 20% 20% 20% 20% 20% 20%
20% 20% 20% 20% 20% 20% 20% 20% 20% 20%

30% 30% 30% 30% 30% 30% 30% 30% 30% 30% 30%
30% 30% 30% 30% 30% 30% 30% 30% 30% 30% 30%

40% 40% 40% 40% 40% 40% 40% 40% 40% 40% 40%
40% 40% 40% 40% 40% 40% 40% 40% 40% 40% 40%

50% 50% 50% 50% 50% 50% 50% 50% 50% 50% 50%
50% 50% 50% 50% 50% 50% 50% 50% 50% 50% 50%

60% 60% 60% 60% 60% 60% 60% 60% 60% 60% 60%
60% 60% 60% 60% 60% 60% 60% 60% 60% 60% 60%

70% 70% 70% 70% 70% 70% 70% 70% 70% 70% 70%
70% 70% 70% 70% 70% 70% 70% 70% 70% 70% 70%

80% 80% 80% 80% 80% 80% 80% 80% 80% 80% 80%
80% 80% 80% 80% 80% 80% 80% 80% 80% 80% 80%

90% 90% 90% 90% 90% 90% 90% 90% 90% 90% 90%
90% 90% 90% 90% 90% 90% 90% 90% 90% 90% 90%

Black Black Black Black Black Black Black Black Black Black
Black Black Black Black Black Black Black Black Black Black

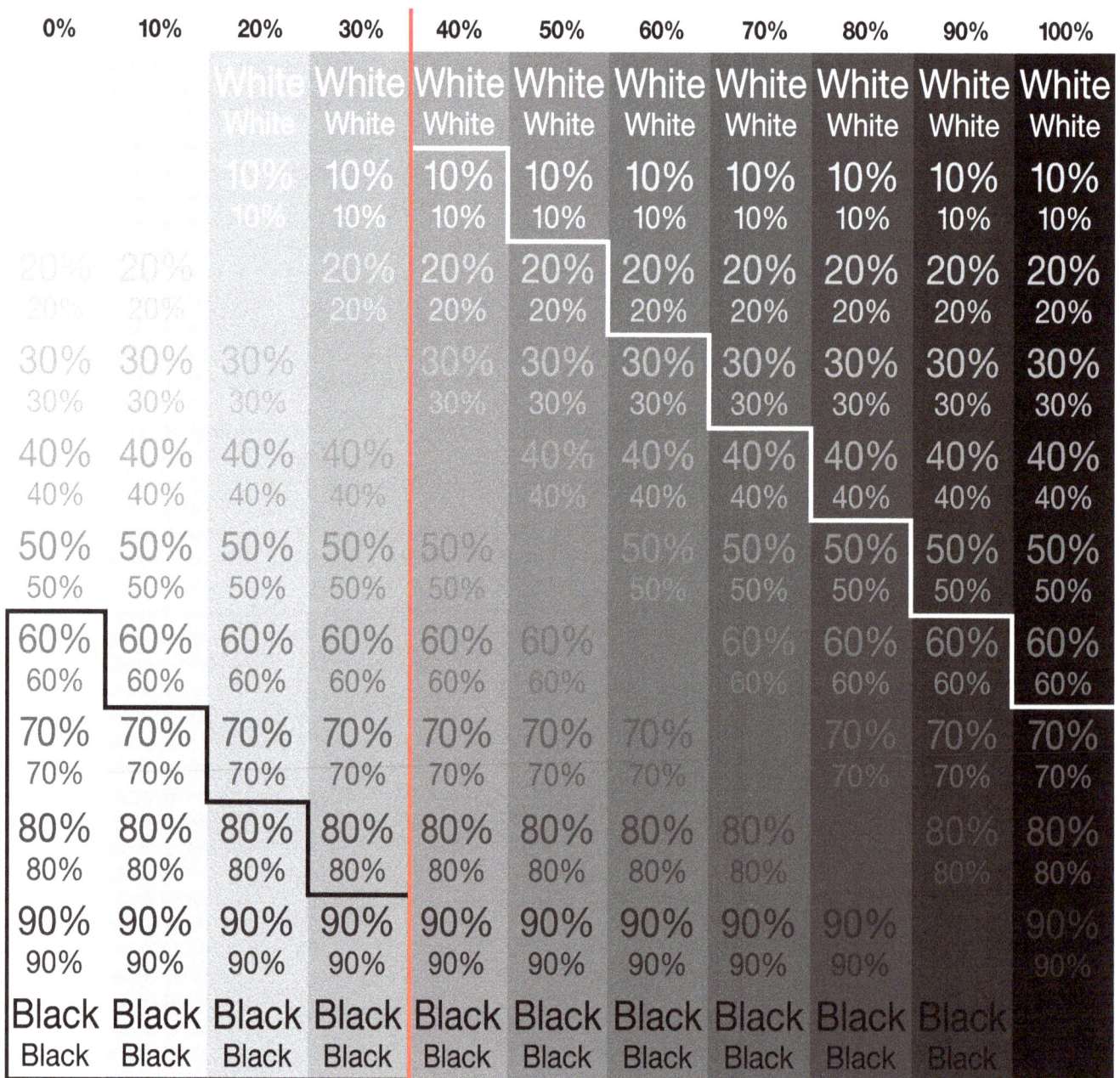

One might expect the cutoff between reversing vs. surprinting to be at the 50% line. But in practice, dark surprinted type over 40% or 50% backgrounds is tiresome, even daunting. Instead, the proper cutoff for reversing vs. surprinting is the 35% mark (red line).

White reflects all available light and black absorbs it. Therefore, white is a stimulus to our visual system, and black is the absence of a stimulus. So when we read black type on a 50% background we are seeing a non-stimulus against a half-stimulus.

On the other hand, when we read white type on the same background, we are seeing a strong stimulus against a half stimulus. That's why it's inherently easier and why reversed type, even at the minimal cutoff, seems to have better contrast. Even so, the 35% minimum contrast is a useful rule of thumb.

In practical application, the cutoff for comfortable surprinting versus reversing isn't at the 50% mark, but at about 35%. Does that strike you as an odd number?

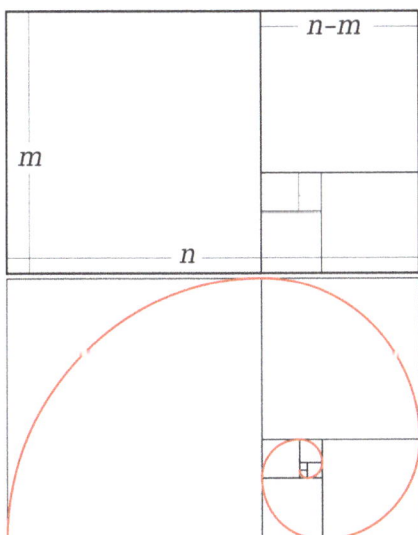

If you begin with a rectangle built with Golden Section proportions, and subtract a square from it, a smaller Golden Section rectangle is left over. Continue doing this and you will get the diminishing series of squares shown at top. If you swing an arc in each square connecting opposite corners, you will create a Golden Section spiral.

Black reflects no light, an abscence of stimulus
Black reflects no light, an abscence of stimulus
Black reflects no light, an abscence of stimulus
White relects light, and is a very strong stimulus
White relects light, and is a very strong stimulus
White relects light, and is a very strong stimulus

It is naturally easier to read white type over a 50% gray background than it is to read black type.

It might, until you remember the Golden Section, the Fibonacci sequence, and its modern counterpart, the Rule of Thirds.

The ancient Greeks discovered a particular proportion that kept cropping up in many different places in nature. They called this the Golden Mean or the Golden Section. They considered it a divine ratio and sought to use it in some of their buildings and sculptures.

Leonardo Fibonacci, a pre-Renaissance mathematician, discovered a sequence of numbers where each adjacent pair

A very similar spiral is found in nature with surprising regularity.

of numbers gave the Golden Section proportion, more or less.

In modern times, photographers and other students of visual arts are often instructed in the "Law of Thirds," which states that compositions will seem most dynamically balanced if major elements are placed within the picture plane at a location of 1/3 or 2/3.

And so it is with the question of when to surprint or reverse. Surprint dark type over backgrounds up to about 35%. Reverse light type over backgrounds from 35% to 100%. In practical terms, there are twice as many colors over which a reversal will work compared to those that will work for surprinting. That's just a fact of visual reality and essential for good contrast.

Now that we've covered the basics of contrast in black and white, we'll cover its application to color next.

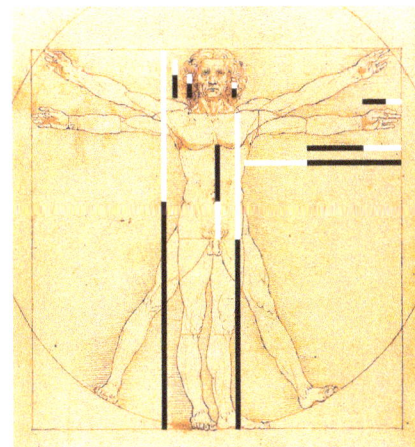

This Golden Section proportions are also found repeatedly in the human body. Golden Section ratios are shown here superimposed over da-Vinci's drawing of ideal human proportion.

Chapter 8

Color and Contrast

Every Color has a Value

Though we may not have thought about it before, every color has a value. By definition, only white can be 0% and only black can be 100%. Merely choosing colors for type that are very different in hue is no guarantee of legibility. It still comes down to value. A designer needs to ignore hue and saturation when selecting colors for type over colored backgrounds. Instead, designers need to learn to consider the inherent value of each color to ensure there is sufficient contrast for good legibility.

SPECIAL NOTE: Given that excellent contrast is 60% differential or greater, it is impossible to achieve excellent contrast over a 50% background.

Designers must always think of colors as values to assure enough contrast differential. Note how marginal contrast in the larger sample becomes more obviously inadequate in the smaller sample.

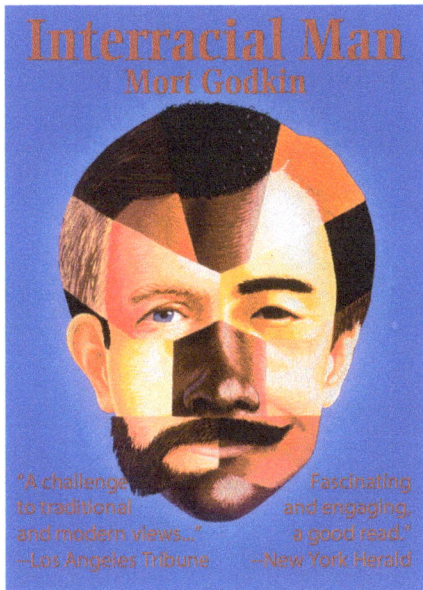

Interracial Man
Mort Godkin

"A challenge
to traditional
and modern views..."
—Los Angeles Tribune

Fascinating
and engaging,
a good read."
—New York Herald

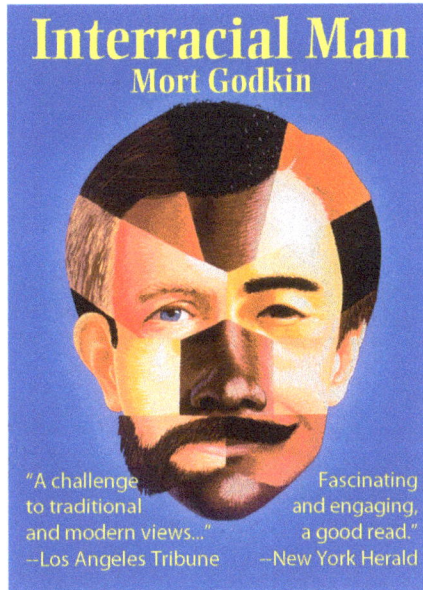

Interracial Man
Mort Godkin

"A challenge
to traditional
and modern views..."
—Los Angeles Tribune

Fascinating
and engaging,
a good read."
—New York Herald

Difference in hue has very little bearing on contrast; only value provides it. And the damage is worse the smaller the type is or if it is lighter in weight. If you think this isn't a big deal, just try to view these covers from even a few feet away. "Interracial Man" by A. Michael Shumate, 1991

In the book covers shown here, we can see that the red type on a blue background is difficult to read in the title and nearly impossible to read in the smaller type. If you browse any online bookseller you'll see how often book cover designers make this mistake, and not just the self-published ones, either.

This contrast issue is made worse the smaller the type is. Now that the majority of books are bought online, the first time most book covers will be seen, they will be only about 150 pixels high.

The Dreaded V Words

If type and its background are close in both hue and in value, the type will vanish as with this magenta type on a red background. If type and its background are close in value but very different in hue, vibrating will occur. While this is more legible than vanishing, it makes up for it by being irritating and should be avoided at all costs.

As with other issues, these are made worse when type is small or being viewed at a distance, such as in signage.

Close values create Vanishing and Vibrating. Both are disastrous to legibility and are worse when viewed smaller or at a distance.

Busy Backgrounds

Type frequently needs to be placed over a photo or other imagery. If the background for type is busy, the type may be impossible to read. Busy backgrounds are defined as those in which both light and dark elements exist.

No color of type will be easy to read over a busy background. Remember, the question is not, "Can the viewer eventually puzzle out what is written?" but rather, "Is this design helping or hurting communication?"

This doesn't mean that a background must always be a flat color. Just make sure that the values are either all light or all dark; only then will surprinted or reversed type will have a chance. However, if parts of the texture are in the mid-value range, it may be impossible to achieve excellent contrast (60% difference or more).

Question: What if the photo doesn't have either all dark texture or all light?

Answer: Time for an assist from Photoshop. :)

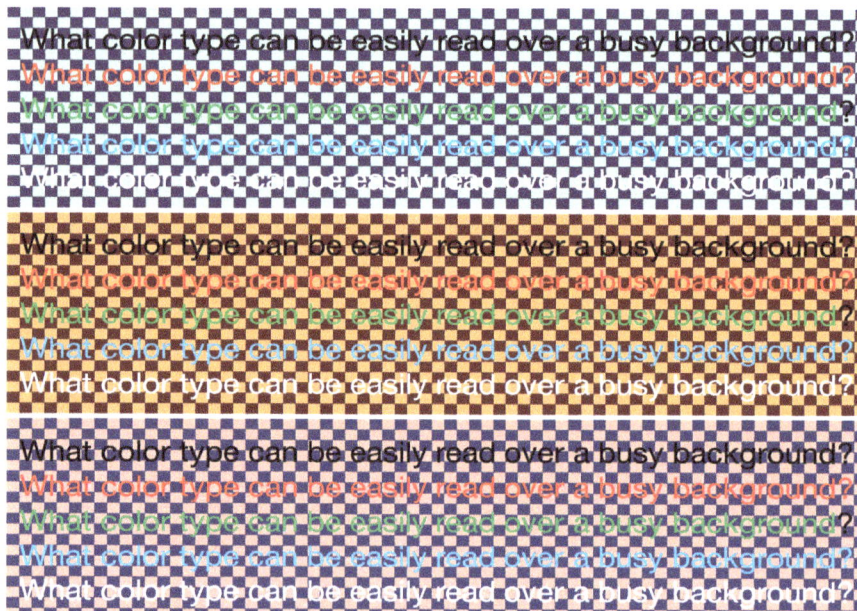

What color type can be easily read over a busy background?
What color type can be easily read over a busy background?
What color type can be easily read over a busy background?
What color type can be easily read over a busy background?
What color type can be easily read over a busy background?

What color type can be easily read over a busy background?
What color type can be easily read over a busy background?
What color type can be easily read over a busy background?
What color type can be easily read over a busy background?
What color type can be easily read over a busy background?

What color type can be easily read over a busy background?
What color type can be easily read over a busy background?
What color type can be easily read over a busy background?
What color type can be easily read over a busy background?
What color type can be easily read over a busy background?

However, if all parts of a background, are either all dark or all light, a good contrast for type can be achieved

However, if all parts of a background, are either all dark or all light, a good contrast for type can be achieved

The text says, "What color type can easily be read over a very busy background?" The answer: Nothing will work. Don't put text over a busy background. Ever.

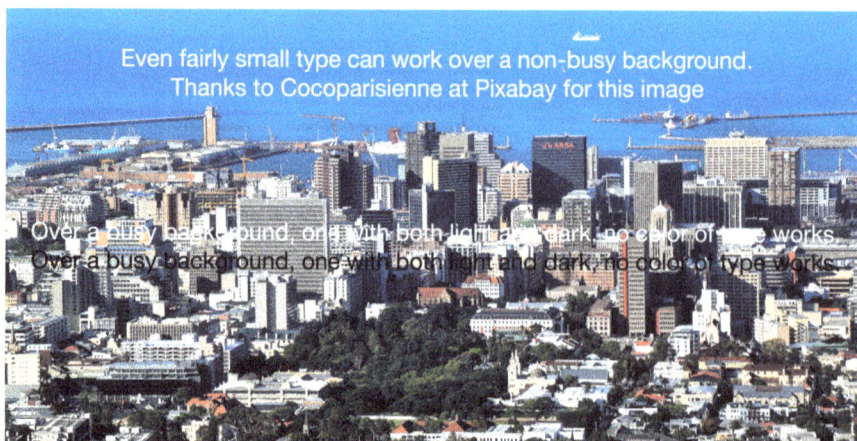

Even fairly small type can work over a non-busy background.
Thanks to Cocoparisienne at Pixabay for this image

Over a busy background, one with both light and dark, no color of type works.
Over a busy background, one with both light and dark, no color of type works.

The text above says over the water, "Even fairly small type can work over a non-busy background. Over the buildings it says, "Over a busy background, one with both light and dark, no color of type works." Thanks to Cocoparisienne at Pixabay for this image."

Widely Varying Backgrounds

A similar problem occurs over widely varying backgrounds, such as over a gradient that has light, mid and dark portions in its progression. Again the answer is: nothing will work well. Some parts will survive, maybe even have quite good contrast, but others will be illegible or at least compromised. Don't do it.

Does that mean that all gradients are useless?

No. But if text is to go over it, then limit the background gradient to the light third or the dark third of the value scale and make the type the other value extreme. For instance, make the background gradient values from about 66% to 100% with light type over. Or else make the background gradient from about 35% to lighter with dark type over.

Remember to avoid colors with equivalent values near 50%. It is impossible to get 60% away from a background with a value of 50%.

What color is easily read over widely varying backgrounds?
What color is easily read over widely varying backgrounds?
What color is easily read over widely varying backgrounds?
What color is easily read over widely varying backgrounds?
What color is easily read over widely varying backgrounds?

What color is easily read over widely varying backgrounds?
What color is easily read over widely varying backgrounds?
What color is easily read over widely varying backgrounds?
What color is easily read over widely varying backgrounds?
What color is easily read over widely varying backgrounds?

What color is easily read over widely varying backgrounds?
What color is easily read over widely varying backgrounds?
What color is easily read over widely varying backgrounds?
What color is easily read over widely varying backgrounds?
What color is easily read over widely varying backgrounds?

A widely varying background is one where both light and dark values are found. No single color of type can give consistently good contrast over such a background. Some part is sure to have poor contrast.

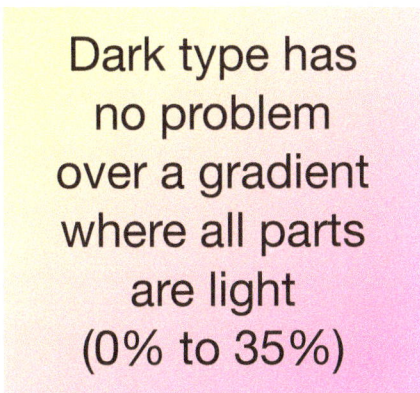

Dark type has no problem over a gradient where all parts are light (0% to 35%)

Light type has no problem over a gradient where all parts are dark (65% to 100%)

Gradients are fine, if you have excellent contrast between all parts and any type going over.

When "Close Enough" isn't Close Enough

In baseball, you get three strikes before you're out. But in graphic design, there are times when two strikes are all you get. Sometimes only one.

Consider outside signage, for instance. It will be viewed in variable lighting conditions. It may have to fight to be seen amid all sorts of visual distraction. The viewer may be moving fast and have only a split-second to absorb the message. I would call outside signage a one-strike situation.

What are other factors that reduce the amount of leeway a designer has? A challenging type font or an unfamiliar or difficult name in the identity can certainly up the ante. Corporate identity is one area where you can strike out with one bad decision, especially when it involves poor contrast.

Anyone who has ever printed from a computer knows that what you see on the screen is often different from what appears on the printed page. Colors can appear too dark, too light, too warm, too cool, too washed-out, compared with their appearance on the computer monitor. Too often beginners think that the contrast in their design, as viewed on the computer monitor, is "close enough." That approach is courting design disaster. One should always consider that the printing (or the viewer's monitor) will eat up some of your "good enough" margin.

But the difference between what is seen on the monitor and what ends up on the page is still variable. *You can't afford to play anywhere near the edge of legibility.* Those who think they are exempt from this principle because they design for

the web are also mistaken because of the inherent difference between Mac and PC monitor gamma (native brightness).

But corporate identity design must be legible in every conceivable output and when viewed in every possible circumstance. Any wise designer will always aim for excellent contrast, which

is a 60% minimum contrast differential or greater.

Don't fudge on those parameters.

These principles are important in all areas of graphic design, but are absolutely imperative in corporate identity design.

Three computer files created by my students were printed on three different printers. The outputs varied wildly. Almost every color printed differently in hue and/or saturation and/or value on each machine, even though they were printed from the *same* computer file and on the *same* brand of printer. No doubt the students assigning these colors thought the contrast as they saw it on their computer monitors was "good enough." You can see for yourself how wrong they were. In each row there are blocks that have type that becomes close to illegible. These contrast errors are magnified when viewed at a distance. Just try stepping back from this page a few feet and see that the words with marginal contrasts become even harder to read.

Chapter 9

The Doctrine of Coincide or Contrast

Here is a principle with many applications in graphic design: elements should either coincide or contrast. It is surprising how often this golden rule of design will answer a wide range of questions—choice of typography, layout, image style and color. We will look only at typography and layout here.

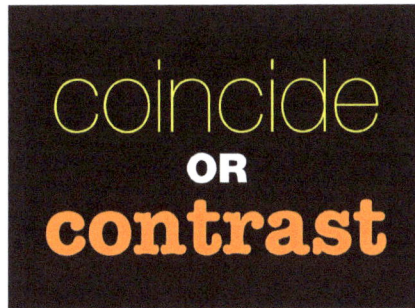

coincide **OR** **contrast**

Font Choices

One of the easiest applications of Coincide or Contrast is in typography. It is very difficult to successfully use two different sans-serif fonts together. There is not enough difference to provide meaningful contrast, but too much difference to coincide.

Getting two different sans serif fonts to work together is very difficult. They don't coincide and they are too similar to contrast.

Helvetica Neue LT Std. Light and Gill Sans Light (same point size).

Perhaps an example in a totally different realm might illustrate. It's like wearing stripes and plaid together; it just doesn't work. Stripes with a plain fabric would give a nice contrast without visual violence. Plaid with a plain fabric could also work.

The same is true when using serif fonts: two different serif fonts are unlikely to work well together. They have too much difference to coincide, but not enough to contrast. They look mismatched because they are. They clash.

The same idea applies to large font families that contain condensed and extended variants. For instance, we should consider Helvetica Condensed or Helvetica Extended to be different typeface designs from Helvetica, because they *are* different font designs. The fundamental shapes of the letterforms have been changed. They can no longer coincide.

Getting two different serif fonts to work together is very difficult. They don't coincide and they are too similar to contrast.

Georgia Regular and Berhard Modern Std (same point size)

This does *not* apply to italic or boldface, which are weight or emphasis alternatives within a single font. They were created to be used together.

While using **bold** or *italic* in the same font are fine for emphasis, using alternate width variants poses the same problem: Not enough contrast but too different to coincide.

Serif Headlines Work With Sans-serif Text

Bold Subheads Can Be the Same Size as Text
Text can be in Roman or Light weight and the same size as subheads. The principle is to have as few type differentiators as your material will support. Remember SIMPLICITY is the soul of good design. Reserve the use of italics for *emphasis* within a block of text.

Sans-serif Headlines Work With Serif Text

Bold Subheads Can Be the Same Size as Text
Text can be in Roman or Light weight and the same size as subheads. The principle is to have as few type differentiators as your material will support. Remember SIMPLICITY is the soul of good design. Reserve the use of italics for *emphasis* within a block of text.

A better alternative is to use either all the same font or a combination of one serif font with one sans-serif font. Then there is enough contrast.

Within a layout, one single font can work very well, with only weight and size to distinguish headlines, subheads and text. Captions are usually offset from body text with size and/or weight variations to differentiate.

Coincide or Contrast in a Layout

Positioning elements is another way to apply the Coincide or Contrast principle. Unless there is a specific reason to do otherwise, aligning your elements will place the focus on the content and not the arrangement, which is as it should be. The purpose of design is to aid communication, not draw undue attention to itself. If elements are only slightly misaligned, it just looks like a mistake.

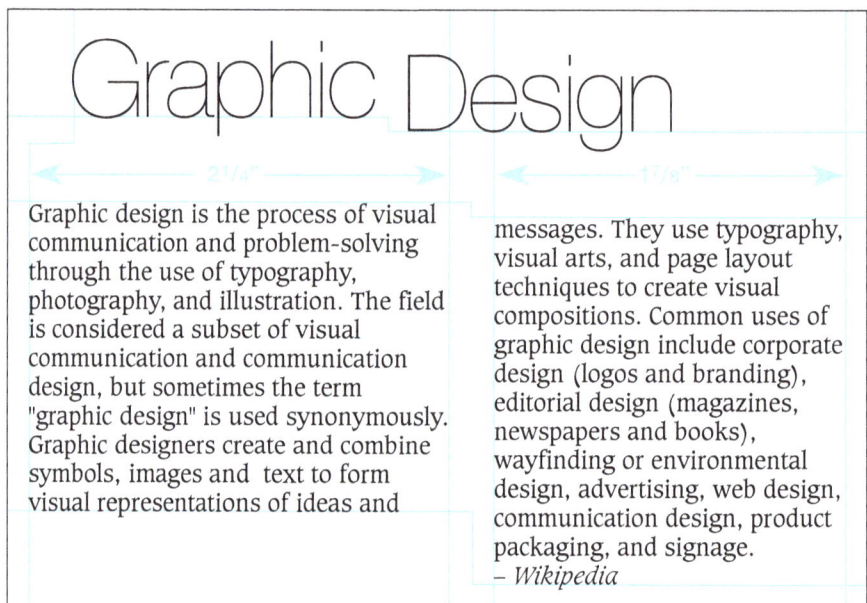

Graphic Design

Graphic design is the process of visual communication and problem-solving through the use of typography, photography, and illustration. The field is considered a subset of visual communication and communication design, but sometimes the term "graphic design" is used synonymously. Graphic designers create and combine symbols, images and text to form visual representations of ideas and messages. They use typography, visual arts, and page layout techniques to create visual compositions. Common uses of graphic design include corporate design (logos and branding), editorial design (magazines, newspapers and books), wayfinding or environmental design, advertising, web design, communication design, product packaging, and signage.
– *Wikipedia*

Now that we've laid a foundation by discussing a few basic principles of design, let's examine the actual subject of this book: Corporate Identity Design.

Branding Fundamentals

Understanding some basics of branding history,
both ancient and recent,
will give us perspective
on branding design today.

Chapter 10

A Brief Overview of Branding History

Branding design is not just a modern pursuit; it has been practiced from the dawn of civilization. Many different approaches have been used, some in media or materials that are not commonly used today. Each method and medium imposed certain constraints on designers.

Cuneiform is the oldest form of writing on earth, dating from about 3000 BC. But even before that—as much as 500 years before—Mesopotamian cylinder seals were in use. These seals were a major inspiration for the development of writing. They were used to identify goods and to sign contracts, and were considered so important that they accompanied the dead in their tombs. Skilled craftsmen made them from hard stones, even gemstones such as hematite, obsidian, steatite, amethyst, lapis lazuli and carnelian. When rolled on soft clay, they left an imprint that was the owner's brand. Their use was legally binding, much as signatures on legal documents are today.

Cylinder seals and the impressions they made in clay. Courtesy of the Louvre

That means that branding is even older than writing.

The Egyptians enclosed the names of their pharaohs in cartouches. These encapsulated names can also be thought of as the precursors of modern logos.

From ancient cultures as diverse as Egypt and China, royal seals not only signified royalty, but also were used to authenticate royal edicts, treaties and laws. This tradition has continued to modern nations, which use them the way corporations use logos.

L to R: 1. Royal Seal of Pharaoh Sahure, c 2500 BC. 2. Egyptian Royal Seal Ring. 3. Imperial Royal Seal of the Great Han Empire c 200 BC. 4. Impression from the Royal Seal of King Henry VIII of England. Courtesy Wikimedia Commons.

Japanese kamon are family crests, and many have been unchanged for centuries. They were used as patterns on armor, flags, swords, clothing and other personal articles. By the 12th century AD, crests were widely used by aristocratic families, and since then have been increasingly adopted by common folk. Many kamon embody principles of modern logo design. The logo for the Mitsubishi Group is a combination of the family kamon of the founder's family and the kamon of his first employer's family.

European medieval heraldry provided identification on the battlefield, where helmets covered knights' faces. Specific symbols and color combinations were placed on helmet decorations, tunics

Aketi	Aoi	Asahina	Botan Chou	Chigai Hishi	Chigai Kuginuki	Daki Myoka	Fukushima
Gamo	Gion Mamori	Gomaisasa	Hanawachgai	Hatakeyama	Hoyo	ii	Inemaru Ni Ichi
Ishikawa	Janome-Shichiyo	Kawari-Itadori	Kikawa	Kiyobucho	Mai-Hou-Ou	Marunidakituno	Matsu
Mituaoi	Mouri	Musubi Kashiwa	Nagagawake	Naruse	Oda	Saigo	Saito
Simikiri Hana	Takanoha	Toda	Toyotomi	Tsugaru	Ume	Yamanouchi	Yotsume

Examples of Japanese family kamon (family crest symbols). There are more than 5,000 such kamon on historical record.

and shields. Elaborate coat of arms designs evolved from these original, simpler designs. Only a single heir legitimately inherited the coat of arms. Non-inheriting sons had to create their own, often variants of the original. Coats of arms were used like modern logos.

Because few people could read in medieval times, signage often had to communicate without words either the nature of a business or the name of a business. A blacksmith sign might show a hammer and anvil; a potter's sign, a mug and pitcher. People who ran taverns and inns tended to choose names that could be illustrated on a sign. This is another centuries-old branding tradition.

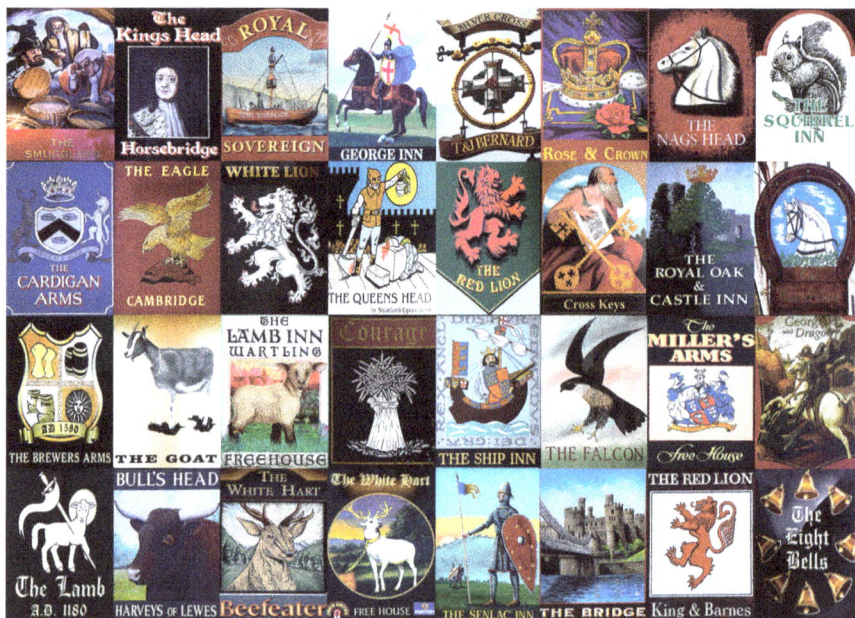

Photos by Roger Medley

Silversmith trademarks, like trademarks from many different trade guilds, were protected by law, with severe penalties for misuse.

Guilds gained strength in various trades by about 1000 AD and enforced quality standards of work among their members, who marked their work to identify each piece. This is the origin of the term "trademark." Trademarking is still practiced for almost all consumer goods.

Producing trademarks in crafts such as silversmithing required considerable mastery. In all cases, it was specialized craftsmen who created identifying devices down through the ages, such as cylinder seals or seal rings.

It is conceivable that apprentices to these craftsmen in each age balked at the stringencies of their respective crafts and wished they could perform their jobs without first mastering such hard-won disciplines. For instance, we can imagine that an apprentice for a cylinder-seal master might propose making seals out of wood instead of the typical hard and unyielding stones. Unfortunately, a wooden seal might not release the clay. Or perhaps a new apprentice might want to employ a fine-lined design "just to be different," only to find that the clay stuck in the little lines and didn't remain in the impression.

There is no getting away from the discipline of each craft. So it is with modern identity design. All around us, people are "designing" unsuitable logos and selling them to unsuspecting business owners, who soon find out that the logos don't work when printed in a single color, or that printing costs are double what they could be with a better design. Some logos can not be perceived clearly from a distance and are therefore useless on a sign. Some can't be shown small on a computer screen because, when rendered through the screen's grid of pixels, they become "pixel mush."

There are ways to avoid these and other pitfalls. The first step is learning the solid principles of branding design.

Next we'll look at some successful brand designs to find out what they can teach us.

Chapter 11

Evolution of Some High Profile Identities

Learning from Others

Nobody can live long enough to learn solely from making one's own mistakes and expect to have learned very much before dying. It is wiser to try to learn from the successes and mistakes of others. It's less painful and learning what works and what doesn't can happen much faster.

Corporate Logo Evolution

The identities of large companies have changed over time, almost always gravitating toward simpler, more elegant designs, and usually conforming to the

Core Principles that will be discussed later in this book. Many companies have a long history of attempting to refine their identity. If we look at their progression from one identity to another and compare, we can see some consistent trends.

These companies have worked hard to get their respective identities just right. Each change represents not only the combined efforts of dozens, if not hundreds, of individuals, but also a massive expenditure of resources.

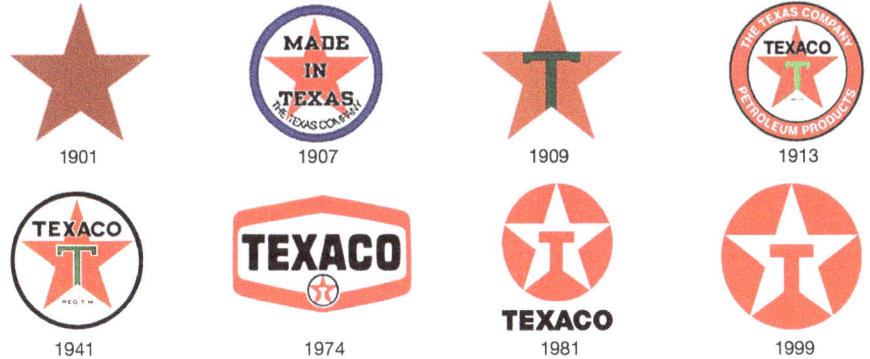

1901 1907 1909 1913

1941 1974 1981 1999

Texaco's identity has been trendy at times, but simplicity and clarity win in the end.

THE WESTINGHOUSE ELECTRIC COMPANY

1886

1900

1921

1936

1960 (Paul Rand)

Westinghouse

Here the progression is ever simpler, cleaner, more direct. Westinghouse changed its logo every 15 to 25 years. Then Paul Rand designed a new logo for Westinghouse, and it has remained virtually unchanged since 1960. Why? Because identities that are designed according to core principles don't become dated.

1900

1904

1909

1930

1948

1955

1961

1971

1995

1999

Rather than becoming harder to recognize by being stylized, if done properly, images become clearer. Beginning with photo-like realism, these logos became increasingly stylized until Raymond Lowey made a perfect Shell logo in 1971. The typography, however, was too trendy and was replaced with a less dated font. Then in 1999 the company omitted the signature portion and used their logo without a signature. Very few companies can ever do that.

| 1876 | 1912 | 1936 | 1937 |
| 1950 | 1956 | 1968 | 2000 |

Through more than a hundred years of evolution, superfluous content is eliminated in the John Deere identity; realism is exchanged for stylization; elements are made simpler and, instead of becoming weaker, become more powerful.

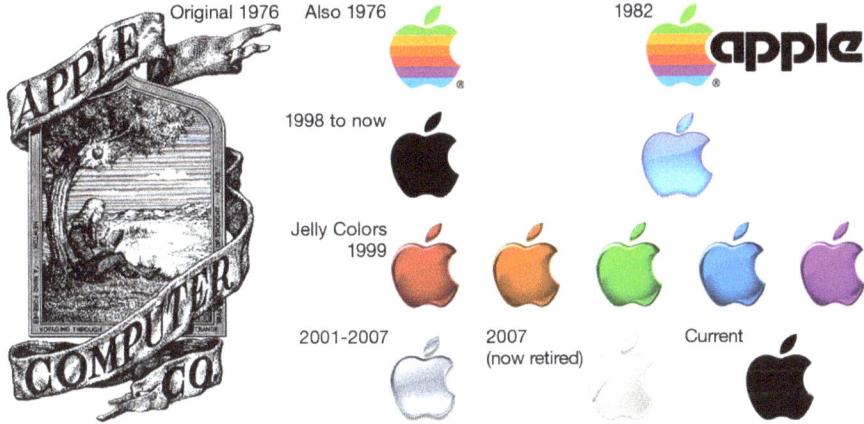

Original 1976   Also 1976   1982
1998 to now
Jelly Colors 1999
2001-2007   2007 (now retired)   Current

The pre-Victorian style of Apple's first logo didn't last even one year. The elegant apple logo was designed in 1976 by Rob Janoff. After that, the rainbow colors were omitted along with the trendy type (such fonts always goes out-of-date quickly). All the changes since then have been treatments; they have been supplemental to the basic flat color logo, but have never replaced it. Even today on the Apple website, it's the simple, one-color logo that is used, not any treatments.

What are the common design trends that these case studies show?

First and foremost, clarity and ease of recognition are paramount. These are absolute baseline requirements. Again and again, these designs prove one overriding principle: nothing can compensate for lack of clarity.

Those who think that clarity is somehow passé are smoking something that's messing with their heads. Without legibility, nothing else matters. If people cannot see and recognize the brand, the design is a failure, pure and simple.

Next are twin qualities that are also indispensable in corporate identity design: flexibility and continuity.

Over and over again we see that simplicity triumphs over complexity, one color over multiple colors, and timeless designs over trendy ones.

Chapter 12

Great Designers of the Last Century

Some designers intuitively worked in harmony with the core principles described in this book. Their logos, consequently, have stood the test of time. They can teach us much. Even the few times when these designers missed the mark can show us that these principles cannot be ignored.

Herb Lubalin, 1918-1981

Herb Lubalin was educated at Cooper Union. During his career he had an affinity for hand rendered typographic identities, which made him an ideal creator of magazine mastheads. Notable examples were the identities for three magazines co-published with Ralph Ginzburg: *Eros*, *Fact* and *Avant Garde*, where Lubalin also did the art direction, often using full-page typographic titles. He created several notable type fonts, including Avant Garde, modeled after the magazine identity of the same name.

He founded International Typographic Corporation (ITC) and left a lasting mark on the world of font design. A memorable publicity tool of ITC's was the free publication *U&lc* (Upper and Lower Case), where he spent the last ten years of his life. It was a showcase of eclectic typographic experimentation. Lubalin's work as a custom typographer often incorporated swashes and ligatures and has been a lasting example of exquisite wordmarks at their best, embracing both simplicity and clarity.

Paul Rand, 1914-1996

Paul Rand was educated at Pratt Institute, Parsons, The New School for Design and the Art Students League but said he was mostly a self-taught designer. He built his early career on the strength of his page layouts, including his ability to crop photos for maximum impact. During his lifetime he was recognized for painting, lecturing and industrial design, but he is remembered today chiefly for his world-famous logo designs most of which still look fresh.

As long as a half-century later, many of those brand designs are still in use and remain essentially unchanged. He continued to be commissioned for high-level identity design into his eighties. More than any other individual of his era, Rand helped big business understand the value of design and of taking graphic design beyond the mere creation of a logo – in fact, toward a holistic design philosophy.

Some criticized his designs as simplistic, but his insight has been proven correct: to have a long life, a good design needs to be simple and restrained. Perhaps Rand's most famous logo is the IBM monogram, originally designed in 1957 and modified by him ten years later and again in 1972. It is interesting that each successive improvement corrected negative issues referred to later in this book. Even the few Rand logos that did not stand the test of time serve to underscore the core principles and how violating them does damage to the utility of a logo.

No matter how famous you are, an identity that doesn't conform to the core principles will be less than effective and is more likely to be replaced.

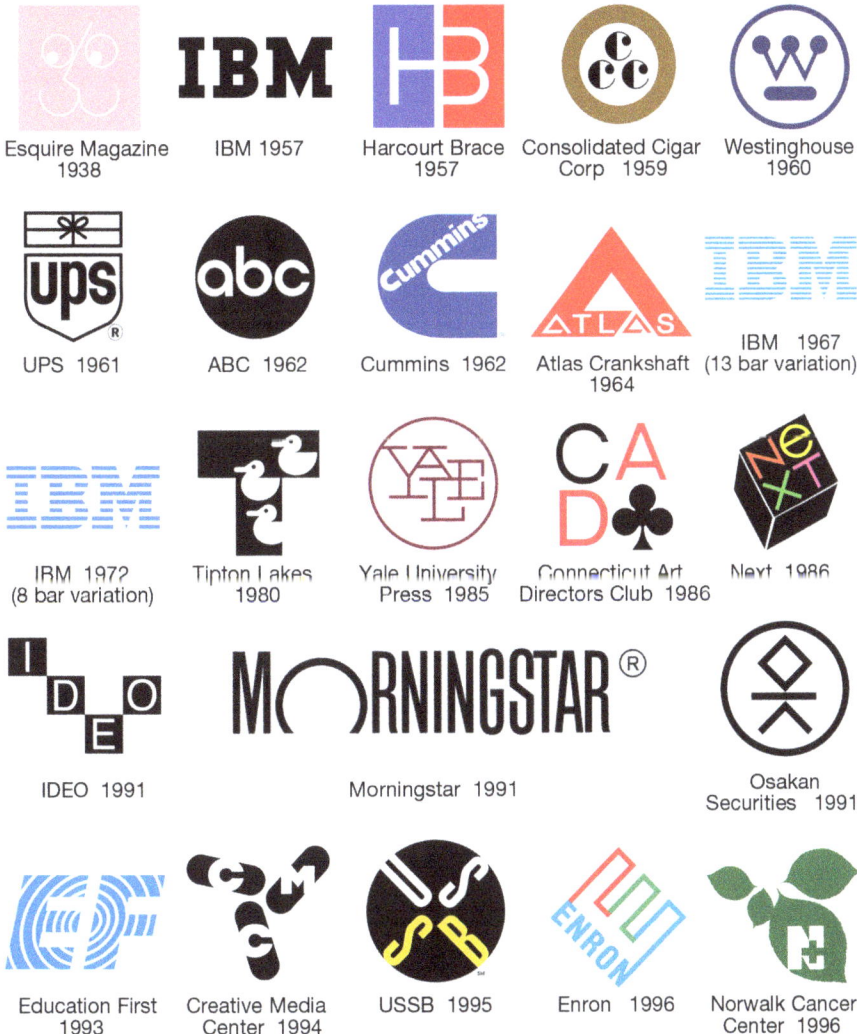

Esquire Magazine 1938

IBM 1957

Harcourt Brace 1957

Consolidated Cigar Corp 1959

Westinghouse 1960

UPS 1961

ABC 1962

Cummins 1962

Atlas Crankshaft 1964

IBM 1967 (13 bar variation)

IBM 1972 (8 bar variation)

Tipton Lakes 1980

Yale University Press 1985

Connecticut Art Directors Club 1986

Next 1986

IDEO 1991

Morningstar 1991

Osakan Securities 1991

Education First 1993

Creative Media Center 1994

USSB 1995

Enron 1996

Norwalk Cancer Center 1996

Saul Bass, 1920-1996

Saul Bass was another graphic designer whose identities have lasted decades without ever looking out-of-date or passé. His design credo was "symbolize and summarize," advice that is still valid today.

After his education at the Art Students League (on a scholarship) and evening classes with György Kepes at Brooklyn College, Bass moved to Hollywood to work on print ads. He produced dozens of film titles for directors like Preminger, Hitchcock, Scorsese and Kubrick, and dozens of movie posters. He also did many book covers and made several

small films, winning an Academy Award in 1968 for his film *Why Man Creates*.

Concurrent with his work in film, Bass distinguished himself in corporate design. Many of his logos remain virtually unchanged today, save for modest variations and treatment alterations. The few logos that were abandoned were mostly victims of corporate mergers or cessations. When

Bass's original designs were replaced, the new ones were almost always weaker and full of shortcomings that will surely mean a shorter lifespan than that of their predecessors. When it comes to companies' retaining logos over time, Saul Bass has a better track record than Paul Rand. This should not be surprising because Bass's logos consistently adhere to the core principles that we'll discuss later.

Lawry's Foods 1959	Fuller Paints 1962	Alcoa 1963	Celanese 1965	Security Pacific Bank 1966
Rockwell 1968	Continental Airlines 1968	Dixie 1969	AT&T Corporation 1969	Quaker Oats 1969
United Way 1972	Ajinomoto 1973	United Airlines 1974	Warner Communications 1974	Avery 1975
Girl Scouts 1978	Minolta 1978	Wienerschnitzel 1978	Boys and Girls Clubs of America 1978	Kleenex 1980
Frontier Airlines 1981	AT&T 1983	US Postage 1983	Kibun Foods 1984	General Foods 1984
Kosé 1991	J. Paul Getty Trust 1993	NCR Corporation 1996	AT&T 1996	

Chermayeff & Geismar & Haviv

Before joining forces, Chermayeff and Geismar were well educated in graphic design. They met at Yale, where Chermayeff earned a bachelor of fine arts and Geismar his master's degree. Originally their firm was a threesome – Brownjohn, Chermayeff and Geismar. Robert Brownjohn left after two years. Since then, the firm has been responsible for more than one hundred identities for companies all over the world and has won virtually every award in the industry. Sagi Haviv joined the firm in 2003 and became a partner in 2006.

Ivan Chermayeff said of the first edition of this book, "...at last somebody understands what identity design is all about and how it is accomplished." Ivan was still an active partner in the firm when he passed away in 2017.

Chemayeff and Geismar (and Haviv after becoming a partner) always worked jointly on all their logo designs. While not all of their logo designs conform to the core principles, the most long-lived ones do. Note that although their logos are reproduced fairly small here, they are clear and solid; and even though they sometimes contain more than one color, each one would work in a single color.

L to R: Ivan Chermayeff, 1932-2017, Tom Geismar, born 1931, Sagi Haviv, born 1974

Chase Manhattan Bank 1961	American FIlm Institute 1963	Mobil Gas 1964	JFK Presidential Library 1964	Burlington Industries 1964
ScreenGems 1966	Merck Pharmeceuticals 1965	Seatrain 1966	Clay Adams 1967	Torin 1968
Xerox 1968	New York University 1972	United Banks of Colorado 1972	Banco de Italia 1973	WGBH 1974
Helaby 1975	United States Bicentennial 1976	National Geographic 1978	Embassy Communications 1981	Lincoln Center 1983
PBS 1984	Koc Holding 1984	E. W. Scripps Company 1985	Rockefeller Center 1985	NBC 1986
Nippon Life Insurance 1988	Univision 1989	Time Warner 1989	HarperCollins 1989	Showtime 1997
Smithsonian Institution 1999	Library Of Congress 2009	Ratpac Entertainment 2013	Avery Dennison 2014	Animal Planet 2018

What does reviewing these famous designers' work teach us?

All of them created some great identities. When they did missed the mark, the typically short life of those identities serves to reinforce the danger of deviating from core principles of branding design.

Chapter 13

Big Brand Agencies and Studios

We have seen that single–or pairs or trios–of visionary designers can distinguish themselves in the field of corporate identity design. There are also big branding consulting firms and larger design studios that have executed many of the brands we recognize today. Typically, there are many designers at work in these larger firms and often their work is a team endeavor instead of the work of a single or small group of principals.

Many of those identities have withstood the test of time and were kept for decades, while other identities were replaced after only a relatively short life.

Some corporations re-brand themselves after a restructuring or merger. A few companies erroneously seem to think it is good business to change their identities regularly, even if their identities are working well. But the majority of companies that change their identities have discovered through experience that their identities are illegible in certain situations, or that they cost more than they should to reproduce or that they begin to look dated. In other words, their identities just don't work like they should.

Most identities that are replaced fall into this latter category. The biggest reason why identities don't work is that they don't conform to the core principles of identity design as explained in this book.

I encourage you to come back to this section and review it after you have learned about the core principles and to see that correlation for yourself.

Unlike preceding examples, where possible, I have placed not only the year of the identity's adoption, but also the year when the identity was replaced by another identity that was substantially different or had significant refinements. While those replacements were not always improvements, it is an indication of those clients' dissatisfaction with the identity as it was. Single dates show when the identity was adopted, indicating that it is either still in use, or was used until some corporate change, such as a merger.

Walter Landor, 1913-1995
and Landor Associates
Born Walter Landauer, in Munich, Germany, he moved to San Francisco in 1939 and founded Landor Associates in 1941. Educated in London before moving to the States, he became, at age 23, the youngest Fellow to date of the Royal Society of Arts. His company has designed identities for hundreds of businesses, including a number for airlines. Many of Landor's designs have lasted for two to five decades and most of those conform to the core principles in this book. Other identities were rather short-lived, perhaps because of the company's earlier tendency to use current or trendy typefaces, which soon become dated. The company has offices around the world and many designers. Lindon Leader began his career working for Saul Bass, then came Landor where he designed the FedEx identity. He now heads Leader Creative.

Delmonte
1963-1991

Bank of America
1969-1998

Levi Strauss
1969-2003

Cotton
1973

Alitalia
1967-2010

Hawaiian Airlines
1974-1990

Thai Airlines
1975-2000

Iberia
1977-2013

Squirt
1978-1988

Tab
1979

US Air
1979-1989

Air Cal
1981

20th Century Fox
1982-1987

SAS
1983-1998

British Airways
1984-1997

Touchstone Pictures
1984

Ahlens
1985-1997

Garuda International
1985

Dole
1986

Philippine Ailines
1986

Sprint
1987-2005

WWF
1988

JAL
1989-2002

Northwest Airlines
1989-2003

Hyatt
1990-2013

Vallo
1991-2002

NEC
1992

FedEx
1994

Netscape
1994-2002

KF
1995

Frito Lay
1997

KFC
1997-2006

Pizza Hut
1999-2014

Verizon
2000-2015

BP
2000

JAL
2002

Meiji
2009

Hertz
2009

DC Comics
2012-2016

Moneygram
2012

BankMega
2012

Jacob's Creek
2014

Comfort Inn
2018

Lippincott

Donald R. Dohner and J. Gordon Lippincott founded Dohner & Lippincott in 1943. It has become one of the world's most successful brand strategy agencies. Based in New York, this firm has also been known as Lippincott & Margulies as well as Lippincott Mercer in the past.

Lippincott has done more solid design work that conforms to the core principles of identity design than any other agency in this chapter, and as a result, have had longer lasting brands.

Xerox
1961-1968

Chrysler
1962-1998

Group W
1963

Citgo
1965

RCA
1968

Chevron
1968-2005

Eastern Airlines
1969

Goldman Sachs
1970

Amtrack
1971-2000

American Express
1972-2018

A&P
1976-2006

NYNEX
1982

Infiniti
1989

Continental Airlines
1991

Samsung
1992

Taco Bell
1994-2016

McGraw-Hill Companies
1995-1999

Skyline Chili
1998

Duracell
1999-1913

Televisa
2001-2016

Sprint
2005

Visa
2005-2014

Delta
2007

Vale
2007

Walmart
2008

TACA
2008

QuickChek
2008

Meredith
2010

Dell
2010-2016

Starbucks
2011

C Spire Wireless
2011

Petco
2011

Ebay
2012

Aviianca
2013

Stanley
2013

Olive Garden
2014

Southwest Airlines
2014

Autotrader
2015

Principal
2016

Bank of America
2018

Wolff Olins

Michael Wolff and Wally Olins founded Wolff Olins in 1965 in London. Since then it has grown to be a large brand consultancy firm with offices in London, New York, and San Francisco.

While they have produced many fine identities that have lasted a long time, they have regularly produced work that has been controversial. It is noteworthy that those identities that have been replaced the quickest are invariably ones that don't conform to the core principles.

Prudential Financial
1984-1989

London Regional Transport
1987-2000

Repsol
1987-1997

BT
1991-1999

Chanel 5
1997-2002

Odeon
1997

Tate
2000-2016

Oi
2000-2016

Vivo
2003

Unilever
2004

General Electric
2004

Telenor
2006

Manpower
2006

Sony Ericsson
2001-2012

Wacom
2008

Tata Docomo
2009

Mercedes-Benz
2009

MapQuest
2010-2012

PricewaterhouseCoopers
2010

Asian Art Museum
2011

Hero Motocorp
2011

Belkin
2012

EE
2012

USA Today
2012

Skype
2012-2017

Univision
2012-2019

Cyient
2014

Enel
2016

Oi
2016

Metropolitan Museum of Art
2016

ZooDoc
2007

Grubhub
2016

Hyatt
2013

Telia Company
2016

Virgin Active
2016

Uber
2018

Pentagram (NYC)
Unlike most of the other companies in this chapter, Pentagram is not a corporation where designers are hired to work for the firm, but a group of individual designers who operate independently, but collaborate with each other, especially on big projects. Designers in this studio have come and gone. When there is a vacancy, the remaining designers will collectively invite a new designer to join their ranks as a full partner, among whom no seniority is observed; it is a collective of equals. Founded in London, it has four offices worldwide, with its biggest studio in New York.

ABB
1988

Victoria & Albert Museum
1988

Electra Records
1989-2004

Fineline Features
1991-2000

Curious Pictures
1993-1999

CNET
1994-2008

Star Alliance
1996

Children's Television Workshop
1997

Citibank
2000

Orbitz
2001-2005

Skyscraper Museum
1997

Nissan
2001

Salt Lake City Library
2009

Saks Fifth Avenue
2007

The Atlantic
2008

Vibe
2008

Bausch + Lomb
2010

Big Ten Conference
2010

Windows 8
2012

Weight Watchers
2012-2015

Billboard
2013

21st Century Fox
2013

Stern
2013

Shake Shack
2015

V Sauce
2015

Verizon
2015

Mastercard
2016-2019

American Express
2018

Yahoo!
2019

Interbrand

John Murphy and his wife opened Novamark in 1974 in New York and changed its name to Interbrand five years later. Now the company has design offices in five other cities around the world.

Of their brands shown here that are over ten years old, over half of them have been replaced or modified.

Deutsche Telekom
1993

Price Waterhouse Cooper
1998-2010

AstraZeneca
1999

Telia
2000-2004

TUI
2001

Opel
2002-2007

Knorr
2004-2019

AT&T
2005-2015

Thai Airways
2005

Holiday Inn
2007-2016

Thomson Reuters
2008

Xerox
2008-2019

Bing
2009-2013

bpost
2010

Porter Novelli
2010

Bankia
2010

Telefónica
2010

NYSE Euronet
2012

Iberia
2013

Sky Network Television
2013-2019

AT&T
2015

Latam Airlines
2016

TIM
2016

Juventus
2017

NSC Comunição
2017

What is the Take-away from All This?

That there are, indeed, core principles of identity design, and if they are violated, an identity will fail in areas where it ought to work. It will be broken in some way and will not serve the client well. Even if the designers don't recognize this, the clients, over time, usually will see it and get a new identity.

These companies employ a wide variety of professionals, from brand strategists to social media masters; from positioning experts to retail and consumer goods specialists. They offer motion graphics and video and packaging and copywriting. And, of course, they have graphic designers who specialize in branding.

But if all of that auxiliary skill is applied to a brand design that does not conform to the core principles, they are building on a flawed foundation.

These companies want to be known as innovators. That may prod them to try things that ought not be done to an identity. What could work beautifully as an app icon, may not work as a brand design. Corporate brand designs may share some characteristics with certain app icons, but they are not the same thing.

This is a book on corporate identity design.

When you consider the logo designs of these companies, there are many excellent ones to point to. There are also some really problematic ones. Each one of these agencies have had designs that just didn't work as identities.

It's seems to be hit and miss.

How can that be in what should be among the most capable branding design firms on the planet?

Because they do not understand the core principles of identity design.

Core Principles

Generating Concepts

Better identities are created
from a position of wealth of concepts
rather than just one or two concepts.
Here is a proven method to develop
more and better corporate identity concepts.

Chapter 14

Corporate Identity Components

Four Identity Components

Before we try to generate concepts, let us stop to remember that there are four different kinds of corporate identity design components. They are:

1) Signatures
2) Wordmarks
3) Monograms
4) Logos

Signatures

As the name implies, a signature is simply a unique way of writing a name. Similarly, brand signatures are corporate names written in a specific font. They have no distinguishing or unique design element added; they are just the corporate name set in a particular typeface or style of lettering.

Signatures are best suited for brand-name consumer products and the corporations that produce them.

Examples are: Alka-Seltzer, Sony, Epson, Daewoo, Clinique, Nintendo and Gillette. This is the most basic form of value-added design, and signatures alone are generally not well suited for identities for other kinds of businesses or corporations.

Originally, the term "signature" meant a personal, handwritten name with natural distinctive characteristics. Interestingly, a signature that is truly distinctive, with a deliberate and individual treatment of letters or a unique design element, is no longer properly called a "signature," but intead it becomes a "wordmark."

Recently, some companies, even in the consumer product category, that formerly had only signatures for their products have added something unique, such as a hand-lettered wordmark or a logo accompanying their established signature.

ELLE
BIRKENSTOCK®
Hertz®
L'ORÉAL PARIS
MICHELIN
ORACLE®

Alka-Seltzer
SONY®
DAEWOO
CLINIQUE
Gillette
Colgate.
AVIS®

EPSON®
DURACELL®
Panasonic.
Chantelle
NIVEA®
CASIO®

CALVIN KLEIN
pandora®
COVERGIRL
DUNKIN'® ebay
RICOH redbox.
heyday™ GUCCI

Signatures are often just a particular font used to spell the functional name of the company. Sometimes the type is hand rendered but it is not obvious and comes across as if all the letters were just a given type font. They are the least value-added in corporate identity design and are most often used for consumer products.

Wordmarks

Wordmarks are sometimes also called logotypes. But some people erroneously say logotypes or wordmarks when they mean signatures or logos. Therefore, because of misuse, the term logotype might well be avoided altogether. For our purposes, plain type "right off the keyboard" (with proper kerning, of course) is not a wordmark; that's just a signature. A wordmark, by contrast, must have some unique design element embedded in the word, perhaps just a type ligature.

The only drawback with wordmarks is that they have just one single format, whereas both monograms and logos, because they are separate from their signatures, can be arranged in different configurations for varying layout needs.

Even so, wordmarks are, and will continue to be, very useful for corporate identity.

What distinguishes a wordmark from a signature is some unique design element or being hand-drawn. Sometimes it is subtle like the tail on the "g" in Ogilvy becoming the dot of the "i." It might be a missing crossbar in the A like in Samsung or the wedges taken out of certain letters in Bridgestone. Other times it can be more obvious like the arched baseline in Netflix or the arrows on Subway.

Monograms

Monograms are a kind of logo that includes or resembles the initial(s) of the company's functional name. Monograms are most often used with an accompanying signature. In the case of IBM or HBO, where the initials have become the functional corporate name and not the words they originally stood for (International Business Machines or Home Box Office), no signature is needed. In these cases, the monogram becomes a coined word or acronym.

Monograms usually contain the first letter or letters of the corporate name rendered in a unique graphic way. The signature spells out the corporate name (Motorola and Hilton). Note that the signature font either contrasts in style with the monogram font (Motorola and Kawasaki) or matches it exactly (Chanel).

Similar but non-matching fonts don't work well. This is the principle of "coincide or contrast" that we have already addressed. Avoid making the monogram the first letter in the signature, as this often interferes with easy reading.

Monograms typically use the first initial(s) in the functional name and are most often accompanied by a signature. Sometimes the monogram letters become the functional name for the company as in the case of IBM and HBO.

48

Logos

Logos are unique design elements that do not resemble letters. They are separate from, but usually used in conjunction with, a signature, type "right off the keyboard" (with proper kerning, of course), which usually has no distinctive design elements of its own. As with monograms, avoid using the logo in place of any letter in the signature as it usually impedes easy reading of the name. In this context the logo and the signature together constitute the corporate identity.

Why This Book's Name?

Even though, for the purposes of this book, I assign separate terms for wordmarks, monograms and logos, the population at large associates the word "logo" with anything that functions as a corporate identity. It is in this context that the title *Logo Design Theory* was given to this book, so that it may be understood by the layperson as well as the professional.

Functional Name versus Legal Name

In identity design, the full legal name is not used. Words such as "corporation," "company" or "Inc." are almost never included. Instead, a shorter name, often just one word, is the functional name used in either a signature or wordmark.

Furthermore, there are some celebrated examples of using the popular name of a company over the formal name. As in so many areas of design, when it comes to the words that must be designed, less is more.

Recognizing that there are only four possible components serves to help a designer cover all bases when developing ideas or concepts, which we'll cover next.

Logos are almost always accompanied by a signature. A logo and signature together become the corporate identity.

Federal Express → FedEx

Advertising Age → AdAge

Whenever possible, it is best to use the simplest name for a company for the Functional Name.

49

Chapter 15

Branding Concepts: Corporate Activity

Design concept is quite different from the issue of identity components mentioned previously. Among all the different logos and corporate identities that you have ever seen, there are only four basic categories of concepts. They are:

1) Corporate Activity
2) Corporate Ideals
3) Corporate Name
4) Abstract

Corporate Activity

These identities show something about the product or the activity of the company. The monogram for Westinghouse, which makes electrical and electronic appliances, is a W that resembles an electronic circuit. The monogram for Allied Van Lines is the letter A, made to resemble a two-lane highway, because Allied Van Lines moves your household belongings "down the road." The logo for tire manufacturer Uniroyal is a stylized tire on pavement. This kind of identity shows what a company does or makes and is, perhaps, the first thing that many designers think of when developing identity concepts. It is a tried and true approach, but it is not the only kind of identity concept and not necessarily the best for every client.

When developing new identity concepts, think of ways to visualize what a company does, and try to make a logo from each concept.

Then, see if each of your corporate activity concepts can be incorporated in the logical initial of the company name, making a monogram.

Next, determine which combinations of activity concepts can be made with the whole word(s) of the functional corporate name. Here, different fonts will allow different possibilities, but avoid fonts that sacrifice clarity for decorative, stylistic or trendy elements. They will become dated most quickly.

If you don't consider how each concept could be incorporated into each of the three possible components, many good possibilities will be left unexplored.

This is only one of the four possible conceptual approaches to a corporate identity. There are three more to follow.

Corporate activity logos illustrate what the company does or makes. Top Row only: The Arthur Ashe Stadium covers the attendees. SwissAir flies you in jets. Allied Van lines takes your stuff down the road. Uniroyal makes tires. Lufthansa flies. Ducks unlimited is all about ducks. This veterinarian cares for pets. Cable TV is self-evident. WWF cares for endangered species like pandas. Burger King has burgers between buns. All of these show something about what these companies do, make or provide to their customers.

Designers need to determine how the corporate activity can be visualized while being combined with the appropriate letterform, which is almost always the first initial(s) of the functional name.

Wordmarks with a corporate activity concept.

Chapter 16

Branding Concepts: Corporate Ideals

Instead of showing what a company does, these identities visualize something about the qualities or ideals to which the company aspires. These can be ideals such as "superiority," "strength," "speed," or "accuracy."

The important thing to remember is that these ideals may not be obvious to the public when viewing the logo but can act subliminally. People don't have to say, "Gee that makes me think of protection and someone taking care of me." But a logo that has a band around something may communicate that on an unconscious level.

Occasionally a double entendre will occur with an identity communicating more than one thing. Those times are serendipitous, but trying to force together multiple concepts can ruin an identity. Doing one thing well is always better than doing two things poorly.

Corporate Ideals Logos: Harris Bank uses a lion, "king of the jungle," for superiority or leadership. Merrill Lynch stockbrokers' logo is a stylized bull; a bull market is a prosperous, growing market, appropriate for a stock brokerage. The Prudential insurance logo is the Rock of Gibraltar, a symbol of permanence; their company slogan is, "As steady as the Rock of Gibraltar." Other ideals might be "love," "softness," "speed" or "fun."

Corporate ideals monograms. A shield can communicate strength or protection; arrows can show action; slanting letters can demonstrate speed. Can you see the skinny B inside the fat B? Other ideals shown are movement, tranquility, friendship, healing, and new beginnings.

AmToy®   Denny's®   LOSS CONTROL   FAITH

PILLOWLINE™   Zenith®   Snugli®   AVANT GARDE

Lee®   Tsop   Ford   iLLCO   Fieldfresh   tear

NORTEL   HILLHAVEN   XCEL   YASA

REDUCTION REVOLUTION   NOT YOUR Father's™   APN'

PARiS   DE ROSA   kiva

Corporate ideals wordmarks. Round edges can convey "safe for children;" odd shapes can say "fun"; straight horizontal lines can show motion.

Chapter 17

Branding Concepts: Corporate Name

These identities do not show either corporate activity or ideals, but the name of the company itself. This approach will work only with certain corporate names.

Wendy's hamburger restaurants do not serve burgers made from little girls, nor does a little girl represent a particular ideal for the company. Instead, the Wendy's logo represents the company's namesake, the daughter of founder Dave Thomas. Petroleum does not come from decomposed sea shells, but Shell Oil's logo is a shell, representing its name. The corporate logo of Apple, the largest technology company in the world, is

an apple, which has nothing to do with either computers or an ideal. Greyhound bus lines, John Deere farm machinery and Whirlpool appliances all use identities visualizing the corporate name directly. Of course, the very shapes of these designs must also be harmonious with corporate ideals and goals, but the logo comes primarily from the name.

Another variation on this concept it to create a mascot, such as the Michelin Man, Julio Pringles, Chester Cheetos, Elsie the contented cow. While not technically a mascot Colonel Sanders has always been the "face" of KFC.

Corporate name logos generally do not depict the activity or the ideals of their companies, but rather the company name alone. Another variant of corporate idenity around the corporate name is to have a mascot as the concept. From Charie the tuna to Mr. Peanut to the Michelin Man, these personifications can become strong brands.

poly

Blue Bunny
ICE CREAM

Air Liquide

The Motley Fool.

seeGRID

BlackJet

Openbank

GREENBIRD

BUILDBOX

Breadfast

HEATGEN

Interlochen
CENTER FOR THE ARTS

These monograms do not tell what the company does or what its ideals are, but illustrate something about the corporate name itself.

Interestingly, there are few situations where the initials of a company's functional name can be shown. Visually representing a name in combination with a monogram should be no harder than other concept/component combinations, but for some reason, good examples of monograms that show the corporate name seem to be more rare than other combinations.

Even though a logo or wordmark showing the corporate name isn't meant to show ideals of the company directly, the style of drawing needs to be compatible with corporate ideals. The greyhound isn't sitting, but running, which is appropriate for a company

SEALED POWER

STAR BANK

heart

echo

slice

CONAIR

6EAR

CONNECT

woo lay
made in wood

Eight

L'eggs

ECLIPSE

ECHO

dialog

Sprouts

starz

BRITISH FENCING

RIOT

nest

AQUATIC

ATLANTIC
GRUPA

These wordmarks all show or describe the corporate name in some way.

that aspires to move people quickly. The apple logo is drawn with precision, not haphazardly or casually, fitting for a company that makes technology products and solutions.

Chapter 18

Branding Concepts: Abstract

Some identities show nothing about the activities, ideals or even the names of their respective companies, but are designed with unique graphic or typographic treatments. Chrysler's five-pointed star inside a pentagram has nothing to do with cars. Neither does Chevrolet's parallelogram. Exxon's wordmark with interlocked "Xs" demonstrates no corporate activity,

ideals or name. And there's no particular overt message in Mitsubishi's wordmark. All of these are abstract.

Even without the psychological ties of the other three conceptual approaches, abstract identities can be effective. However, the shapes of abstract identities must still be harmonious with the nature of the company and its ideals.

Abstract Logos

Litton

HUBBARD

McCULLOCH

Delco

VW

DAK

TRW

GM

weyel
international

UNIVISION

M

HEWLETT
PACKARD

MAYTAG

bitcoinlive

H&M

HBO

Manulife

RCA

DÆHLIE

FWM
FORT WORTH MUSEUM
SCIENCE AND HISTORY

McGrathNicol

Harvard
University
Press

zendesk

Naylor
Love

Oxford
Dictionaries

MARINGA FC

THE
ELIZABETH TAYLOR
AIDS FOUNDATION

JOHN MUIR
HEALTH

Royal Conservatoire
of Scotland

Dentsply
Sirona

MUSÉE DE LA
CIVILISATION

ART WORKS.

Nuvance
Health

Portland
State
UNVERSITY

joods
cultureel
kwartier

HYUNDAI

Abstract Monograms

58

EXXON   EXCEL.   TYCO   Allstate®   VOX

INTERPLAK   Liquitex®   Ford   USLIFE   Oster

NYNEX   FedEx.   AMETEK   THERMOS

digital   Mobil   SHERWIN Williams   USWEST

Alitalia   makita   CASE   Sunbeam

ESPN   vimeo   Wilson.   STANLEY.

tibi   SECTIGO   designmodo   VISA

Coca-Cola   CATERPILLAR   RE/MAX®

Abstract Wordmarks

Now that we've covered the three
possible identity components and the
four possible concept approaches, what
do we do with this information?

Chapter 19

Knowing Your Client

You will create your best designs when you understand your client's needs—and even better, when you understand the needs of your client's customers, because they are the real audience for any corporate identity. In our profession, a designer must become an "instant expert" in various companies. This is a challenge, but it is also one of the perks. How can you get bored when you must think like an accountant one day, an industrialist the next and a service worker after that? For a designer of corporate identities, it's never "same old, same old."

But this "inside" knowledge doesn't come without effort. The easiest way to learn it is directly from your client.

Interviewing Your Client

Here is a sample of questions that can help you understand your client and thier customers:

• What is this company's activity?
• Specifically, what do you do? What is the essence of this business?
• What is the product of your business? What do your customers get from your product or service? Digging deeper, what is the final benefit, advantage or improved state of being that using your product or service gives the customer?
• What objects or images have been associated with your company's products/services in the past?
• What objects or images could be associated with your company's products/services?
• What are the major competitors for your business or alternatives for your customers?
• What niche or characteristic makes your company unique?

• What qualities, feelings or ideals would your company like associated with it? (see Discovering Appropriate Ideals Activity)
• What sort of imagery could convey those ideals?
• What qualities, feelings or ideals would your company NOT want associated with it?
• What sort of images might be associated with your corporate name?
• What kinds of imagery are compatible with your company's character, specialties and marketplace niche?
• How do you want your business to grow?
• What kind of clientele do you want to attract? Will this be a new market or greater share of your existing market? Is it domestic, business to business, industrial, international?
• What are some of the jargon words used in this industry for things like the customer's problem, a job well done, and so on?
• Comments / Questions / Clarifications

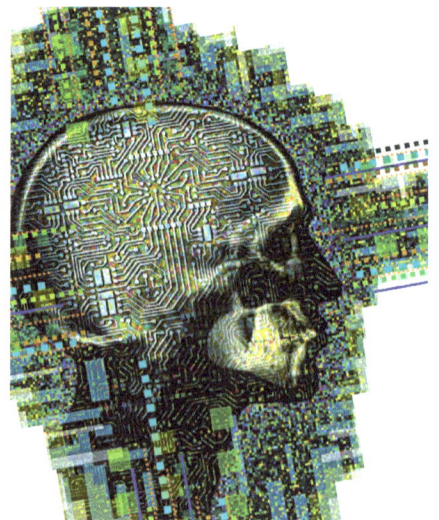

Discovering Appropriate Ideals

As part of a designer's interviewing of a client, the following exercise may be helpful. This will obviously inform corporate ideals concepts but will also help the designer choose shapes for executing *any* concept.

1. From the list of words in the following block, underline any word that *should be* associated with this company.

2. Put an X through any qualities with which your company would avoid association.

3. Go back through the list and circle the five *most important* definers of this company's desired reputation.

4. It is quite likely that by going through the following list of words, other words that may be more appropriate for your client will emerge. Feel free to add words at the bottom of the grid that better fit qualities or ideals that your company would want, or would not want, to be associated with.

Ideals

expansive	coalescing	divergent	moving	focus
open	strong	fast	accurate	random
serious	juvenile	easy	difficult	solid
soft	professional	fluid	fun	technical
caring	delicious	durable	educational	loving
outward	inward	protective	steady	concluding
communicative	contemporary	liberal	conservative	modest
coming together	beginning	purity	leading	natural
economical	rich	traditional	high-tech	smart
feminine	masculine	casual	responsible	growing
protective	exciting	becoming	entertaining	healthy
illuminating	royal	achievement	activity	adaptable
consistent	in command	competitive	connected	analytical
fairness	finding	contextual	deliberate	disciplined
developed	empathic	futuristic	harmonic	creative
inclusive	individualistic	accepting	old fashioned	intelligent
maximal	positivity	relating	restorative	secure
strategic	fragrant	economical	first-class	impartial
superior	friendly	exact	honest	reliable
_____	_____	_____	_____	_____
_____	_____	_____	_____	_____

Chapter 20

Self-Brainstorming

Brainstorming

This is a term coined by advertising executive Alex F. Osborn for group co-operation in generating ideas. Three basic principles govern successful brainstorming:

1. All judgement is deferred to later.
2. Idea quantity is the goal.
3. Unusual ideas are valued, as are combined ones.

For this to work in a group, no participant comments verbally or otherwise on any idea expressed. All ideas are recorded. This maxim prevails: "Quantity Breeds Quality." It is only later that the ideas are evaluated or sorted critically.

One successful variation on this technique is called directed brain-storming. Each participant is asked to write one idea on a piece of paper. The papers are shuffled and exchanged, and each participant is asked to come up with a new idea that improves on the one already on the sheet. Participants again

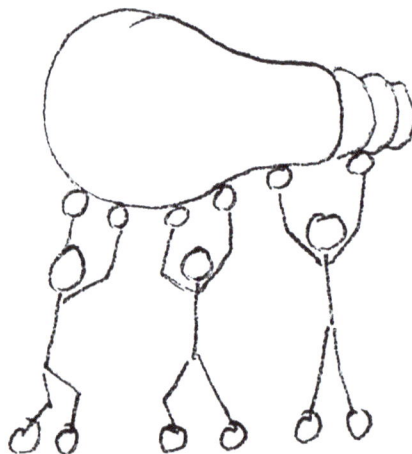

Ideas can come from many places. Since making sure that each and every idea captured is essential, our stick people shown here are particularly appropriate.

swap pages, and add improvements for another few rounds.

We'll look at these techniques and see how they apply to generating corporate identity concepts on your own.

Left Brain, Right Brain

It is a popular notion that the two hemispheres of the human brain have divergent capabilities and inclinations, in addition to controlling opposite sides of the body. Generally speaking, the left side is credited with being the analytical, verbal/linguistic and logical side of the brain. The right side is thought to be the spatial, visual and creative side. Typically, the belief is that both sides can't work on their respective specialties at the same time.

Modern brain research does not support this concept. Instead, it shows that capabilities like speaking are dependent on various specific areas of the brain, each with different contributions to the whole process. It also shows that most processes are not exclusively left-brain or right-brain functions. While the pop wisdom about left and right brains isn't completely true, the idea that different parts of our brains do different things is validated.

With that caveat in mind, and still using the model that the right side of the brain is the creative side, we might suppose that conceptualizing and designing corporate identities should be largely a right-brain activity, right?

Wrong.

Why would we think that half a brain could do a better job than a whole brain? Is there a way to get multiple parts of our brains working together synergistically?

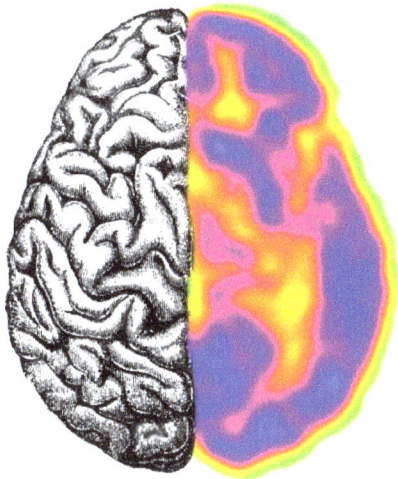

Even though it is not a scientifically accurate model according to the latest research, the left brain/right brain concept is still useful for this conceptualizing exercise.

Yes.

Visualize the four kinds of identity concepts as an outer ring of a wheel that can revolve around an inner circle that contains the three kinds of identity components. You can use this wheel to generate more ideas. Each identity component can work with any of the four identity concepts. Since signatures have no concept at all other than font choice, they don't show on the inner

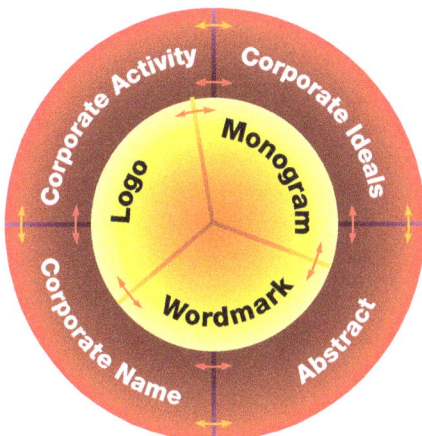

circle (but are still needed to accompany a logo or a monogram).

You should try to have at least one or two of each of the following combinations:

- Corporate Activity Logos
- Corporate Ideals Logos
- Corporate Name Logos
- Abstract Logos
- Corporate Activity Monograms
- Corporate Ideals Monograms
- Corporate Name Monograms
- Abstract Monograms
- Corporate Activity Wordmarks
- Corporate Ideals Wordmarks
- Corporate Name Wordmarks
- Abstract Wordmarks

Rather than the left brain getting in the way of the right brain, one side can act as a catalyst for the other. Instead of stifling creativity, this approach can promote it. Correctly practiced, this kind of conceptualizing can put any designer in the position of working from a wealth of good concepts. Instead of trying to come up with a single good idea, the designer might have to decide which of the good ones is the best. That's where we all want to be.

As you consider each idea, write it down and draw a quick thumbnail to record it. *Every idea*, not just the "good" ones. By considering each of the four different kinds of concepts, you are getting the left side of your brain to collaborate with or jump-start the right side. Later, every thumbnail or sketch can also help pollinate new ideas.

Working the Technique

Be sure to take notes when interviewing your client. Single words or phrases can be crucial. After reviewing your interview notes, ask yourself the same questions, but don't be content only with the client's answers. An experienced set of outside eyes may see things that the client doesn't. So when you ask yourself the following questions, see if you can come up with the most accurate and useful answers.

- What is this company's activity?
- Specifically, what does it do?
- What is the essence of the business?
- What objects or images can relate this company's products or services?
- What niche (such as quality, speed or price) makes this company different from its competitors?

Ask yourself all the questions you asked the client and put your answers, if different, in a different color in the margins of your client notes. Compare them. Try to articulate why you had any answers that vary from the client's. Note those things too.

Some of the answers may lend themselves to more than one of the conceptual approaches. For instance, something might be interpreted as the company's activity or the company's ideals. It doesn't matter which slot it gets categorized in. What matters is that the concept was generated, and became a tangible idea.

Make written lists of objects that can represent, or be associated with, the corporate activity. Make initial sketches of those objects.

Then take it a step further. Think how these concepts might be shown in a less-than-literal way. Some designers tend to be too realistic in producing an image. Logos are *not* illustrations and certainly not clip art. Back off. Instead of being confined by a literal likeness, try to merely suggest the object in question. Many of the best corporate identities have this less-than-literal quality.

Next, consider ideals that the client might legitimately aspire to or, conversely, which qualities or ideals might be antithetical to the client's image. After determining the top five company ideals, think of ways to represent them. What symbols might you use? A lion can represent superiority or royalty as well as strength. A flower can represent love, freshness, growth. Lines slanting to the right or arrows can mean forward motion and speed. Hearts, eagles and crowns are all images that communicate ideals. There are thousands of possibilities.

Is there a way to visualize the company name, perhaps with a mascot? Many company names are family names of the founder, but often those surnames have meanings that could be visually represented. Sometimes the logo can show how to pronounce the company name (such as the bear profile logo for Behr Paint). Always look up a company name in the biggest dictionary possible or an online dictionary that will define non-English words as well. Wikipedia defines a surprising range of surnames.

The term "abstract" conveys a lack of associations. That doesn't mean that any old image will necessarily work for a given logo. What graphic shapes are naturally compatible with the corporate activity or ideals without actually representing them? The Chevrolet logo doesn't look like a car but has been a

"Working Brain" by A. Michael Shumate, 1990

very effective abstract logo for more than a century.

You haven't done a complete exploration of conceptualizing until you have come up with a few ideas associated with each of the four identity concepts on the outside of the wheel, combined with each of the three components on the inside. It may be difficult to focus your

Sketch every idea. No slacking. Don't edit or evaluate. Later, a poor idea might just have a shape or an element that will be the key to a truly memorable design. Original image of hand courtesy Tolga Kocak. Freepik.com

brain to each combo, but the exercise will bear fruit, be assured.

In effect, this technique allows you to brainstorm with yourself. During a proper multi-person brainstorming session, evaluations are not allowed. The object is to get as many ideas as possible on the table or on paper and do the sorting later. It should be the same for you at this stage. Resist the temptation to evaluate while in the act of generating ideas. Let the flow happen.

Evaluating from a Position of Plenty
With a basket full of ideas, the designer can turn off the idea stream and put on a different hat. Now each idea can be examined. If a single concept seems inadequate, see if two concepts can be merged, as long as the concepts are compatible. Even those ideas that may look useless, overused or trite, in combination with some other element, may become a truly remarkable design.

With some practice, this technique will produce several good ideas, from which the very best can be selected. Conversely, designers who stop at one or two ideas cannot afford to evaluate them too closely because they have not developed the ability to generate ideas on demand. But when generating ideas no longer is a major hurdle, attention can then be directed to developing the greatest ones, instead of the merely adequate ones.

Two Warnings:
1. Don't conceptualize on the computer. Use a pencil for quick sketching.

2. Later, when combining and refining ideas, don't draw lines but solid shapes. This will be understood better after we discuss the Seven Deadly Sins of Logo Design.

Core Principles

Seven Deadly Sins of Logo Design

Several common approaches to identity design
that prevent an identity from working
in ways that every identity should be able to work.

Chapter 21

The Seven Deadly Sins of Logo Design:

Blowout

Use of Branding

For most readers of this book, the word branding conjures up images of logos, ads and labels. But agricultural branding of cattle practiced today is millennia old. It didn't start with cowboys in the Wild West; it dates all the way back to ancient Egypt.

Not only was its purpose the same as it is today—to identify whose cow was whose—but the nature of those brands was similar to modern cattle brands. They were fairly simple, and they had to be easily recognized.

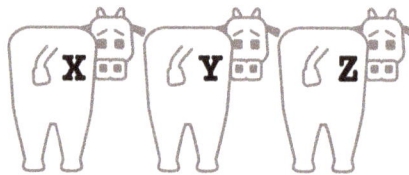

The purpose of a cow brand is similar to a corporate identity or brand in modern marketing: to identify the owner.

Imagine a dude who has gone out West to be a cowboy. He designs a new brand for his cows that's unlike any of the others being used—"just to be different." The old-timers tell him the brand won't work, but he doesn't listen. The young dude answers, "You're just jealous because my brand is distinctive, innovative, ahead of its time. Well, isn't that the whole purpose of a brand, to be unique?"

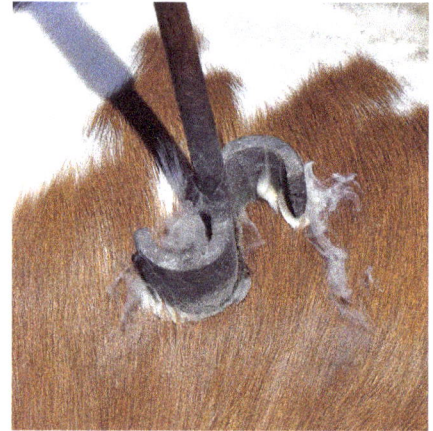

What good is a cow brand that can't be read from a few feet away, if the design gets obscured by nearby hair or when the cow is wet? Photo courtesy of Searle Ranch.

So this dude proceeds to brand all his cows with his new "innovative" brand design. But the shapes are so fine that the nearby hairs cover the brand. And when it rains, and the cow gets wet, it can't be seen at all.

Yes, it is new and different, but it isn't a very good brand design, is it?

Now imagine you are buying a used car and the salesman says something like this: "Just don't drive it in the rain. Don't take more than two people in it at a time. Oh, and the brakes don't work in cold weather. Aside from that, it's a great car!"

You would probably shop elsewhere.

Lazy Design

The idea that the lack of a little care can lead to big disaster isn't new. The centuries-old proverb "For the Want of a Nail" is a perfect example of a little neglect having big consequences.

> For want of a nail,
>   the shoe was lost;
> For want of a shoe,
>   the horse was lost;
> For want of a horse,
>   the rider was lost;
> For want of a rider,
>   the message was lost;
> For want of the message,
>   the battle was lost;
> For want of a battle,
>   the kingdom was lost.
> All for the want
>   of a horshoe nail.

If the proverbial nail was missing due to abject poverty, it would be unfortunate. If it was just wear and tear, we could chalk it up to fate. But if the missing nail was an act of carelessness, then its absence is truly tragic.

Too many designers don't know the serious errors that can be made in identity design. But even worse, some don't care. They don't care that the client won't get full utility out of the identity they've designed. For them, the pursuit of "cool" trumps the creation of an effective identity.

That's lazy design.

Design isn't brilliant because it's different; it's brilliant if it works beautifully in all situations.

Design isn't **brilliant** because it's **different**; it's **brilliant** if it **works beautifully** in all situations.

Sadly, our design publications are filled with identities that are touted as being new and different but will utterly fail at their fundamental purpose—being seen and recognized or being reproduced in a variety of situations. No wonder so many designers today have no clue what good identity design is.

One of our original premises in this book is that a professional always acts in the client's best interests. Therefore, a designer's first responsibility is to create an identity design that will meet all the requirements necessary: to be clear, recognizable, and reproducible and consistent on all of the client's desired presentations—signage, vehicles, business forms, ads or websites.

Imagine a designer meeting with a client to present an identity and, after unveiling the design, says, "This is a cool design, but people will have a hard time seeing it on your vehicles. And you'll need to make it at least an inch-and-a-half tall on your website for good clarity. Oh, and by the way, it won't photocopy or fax well at all. And forget about it looking good in the Yellow Pages."

Sound far-fetched?

Sad to say, thousands of clients have paid so-called professional designers for work that has just those kinds of limitations. The worst part is that neither the clients (understandably) nor the designers (shamefully) had enough foresight to predict this.

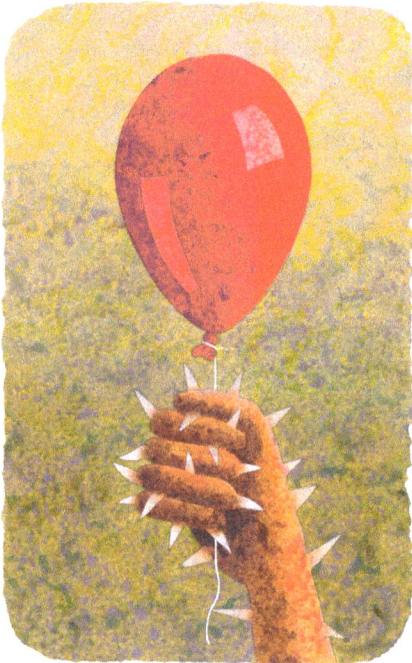

Let's take this in a different direction. How many holes can a balloon have before it pops? How many holes can your car's gas tank have before it's a threat? (And we're not talking about the input line or the fuel line to the engine, either.) How many holes can a tire have before it has a blowout?

Photo courtesy TireZoo.com

The correct answer in all three cases is "just one." It takes only one hole in each situation to pose a serious problem.

Too many who claim the title of designer have no clue what their "lack of a nail" will cause. A poorly designed identity could double or triple certain reproduction costs. It could simply not work on signage or when the identity has to be used small. It could reflect poorly on the client because of sloppy rendering. It could just be insipid and weak.

Seven Deadly Sins

It may strike some as overly melodramatic to use the term "Seven Deadly Sins" to describe shortcomings in logo design. Perhaps so. However, our look at the history of several corporate identities shows us that companies will and do get rid of identities that don't serve well. Sometimes it's due to corporate takeovers or other changes in corporate structure, but more often these companies simply realize that the current identity just "doesn't work" in one or more situations. Given the massive expenditure that revising a corporate identity represents, smart companies obviously want a corporate identity that always "works." Trial and error does eventually yield better results, but it's a terribly lengthy and expensive process.

Wouldn't it be easier to look at other people's mistakes and simply avoid those same mistakes?

Some might feel that such restrictions stifle their creativity, but if the goal is to get somewhere, why not take the route with the fewest pitfalls and dead ends?

I propose that there are indeed seven errors in identity design that are like that fatal hole in the balloon or the tire. If any identity doesn't work in the way it should, it's busted.

It's broken.

It's a blowout.

Chapter 22

Deadly Sin of Logo Design #1:

Can't Work In Solid Black

Every identity ought to be able to work in one single flat color, like black. Even if black isn't the official "corporate" color, if the design doesn't work in black, it doesn't work.

Too many think this has no relevance today. They think that, in this day of computer graphics and the Web 2.0 look, such notions are archaic and passé. But lest I come across as a grumpy design curmudgeon with backward or retro ideas, look at the innovators of that very Web 2.0 look. What company has led the way in industrial design and digital utility more than any other? What company epitomizes contemporary design and refinement in everything from advertising to packaging to product design?

Apple.

Some might ask, "Doesn't Apple have a logo that employs that cool transparent glass or jelly look?" Yes, but it is based on their solid black design. In fact, the company still uses the solid shape—not the Web 2.0 version—on all its products. Go to the Apple website. Do you see the transparent jelly version of the Apple logo anywhere? No. In fact, how big is their logo? Only 31 pixels wide! Try doing that with a logo whose *only* version has a color jelly or transparent look.

The issue isn't that the glass look is wrong. It's just that the transparent or dimensional look is *not where you start*. You start with a solid design, and add the whistles and bells afterward. You don't design something that is all whistles and bells but has no substance. And that won't change, even when we're at Web 100.0.

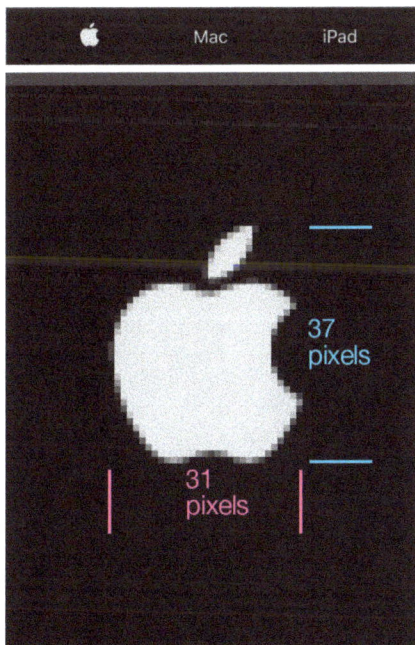

Here (top) is the Apple logo as seen on their website, and enlarged ten times so you can see that it is only 31 pixels wide and 37 pixels high.

With a solid, well-designed identity, you can always embellish it. There's no problem beautifying a solid shape. But the opposite is not always true. Start with the 3D, multicolored, or transparent version, you may find nothing substantial under all the effects.

You can always embellish a solid design. But when you start with an embellishment, there may not be a solid design underneath it.

Regrettably, too many identities are designed this way, and not just for companies that couldn't afford the best design. In fact, some huge companies have paid hundreds of thousands of dollars to rebrand themselves with identities that are weaker than the brands they replaced. As if that were not bad enough, they then spent more hundreds of thousands of dollars, sometimes even millions implementing that new weaker brand on their vehicles, signage, stationery, and their products themselves.

Ignorance about this principle is rampant in the graphic design industry today.

Photographs and illustrations do not make for good logos or identities. There are too many subtleties that just don't translate into different media and at the sizes where a properly designed logo should be able to survive. Photographs can't be reproduced faithfully in cut vinyl for vehicles and signage. One might counter that we now can reproduce photos in vinyl. True, but they don't last as long as cut vinyl. For companies with large vehicle fleets, this translates into significantly more expense over time. But even more common processes, like photocopying, will compromise the clarity of a photo or illustration masquerading as a logo.

Some designers think gradients are acceptable for identity design, reasoning that halftones will reproduce them well. That may be true for magazines and brochures, where the printing quality is relatively high, but what of the

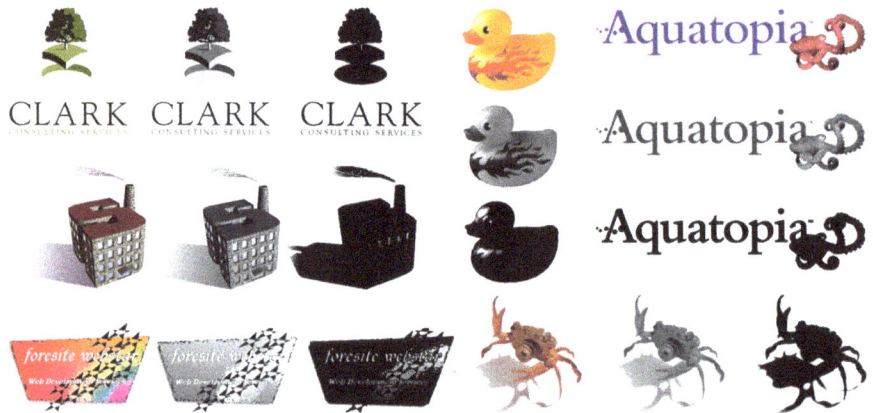

Here we see some recent multi-color illustrations that have been apssed off as logos. After taking away all the color, most of them are wimpy at best. When you render them in black only, as in a photocopy, they are almost unrecognizable. Sadly, most of these were featured in design annuals as good examples of logo design. They are not.

smaller printing presses used for most companies' stationery reproduction? Beyond that, newspapers and the Yellow Pages do poorly with halftones. Because of their poorer paper quality, a coarser dot-per-inch halftone is often used where gradients can end up looking blotchy.

Color is a beautiful thing, but even

Gradients may disguise the inherent weaknesses of certain designs. How many of these have the internal contrast to provide excellent legibility? Rendered in solid black, they fail altogether.

when using flat colors in identity design, multiple colors can mask the lack of a fully developed core design. Too many colors can be a crutch. Ask yourself, "Can the design walk without the crutch of color?" The very word "design" implies finished forms, not half-baked shapes that must have color to work.

In many of our modern media, such as magazine ads, internet, TV and packaging, full color is the norm, with no extra cost for a multi-color identity. But this does not mean a logo will always have full color. In many other formats—including stationery, everyday business forms, signs and vehicle identification—needing to show a multi-color identity will significantly increase costs by 150 per cent, 300 per cent or even 400 per cent. Persuading clients to buy into those extra costs, without having warned them beforehand, is extremely unprofessional. It is amazing how often this happens. Clients may not think of the reproduction difficulties that a particular logo design can present. That is not their job. But it *is* the designer's job to think ahead and to be professional enough to at least give clients a choice.

Very few multicolored designs are so wonderful that an alternative design that works as well in solid black would not have been preferable.

Every identity design ought to be able to work in a single flat color.

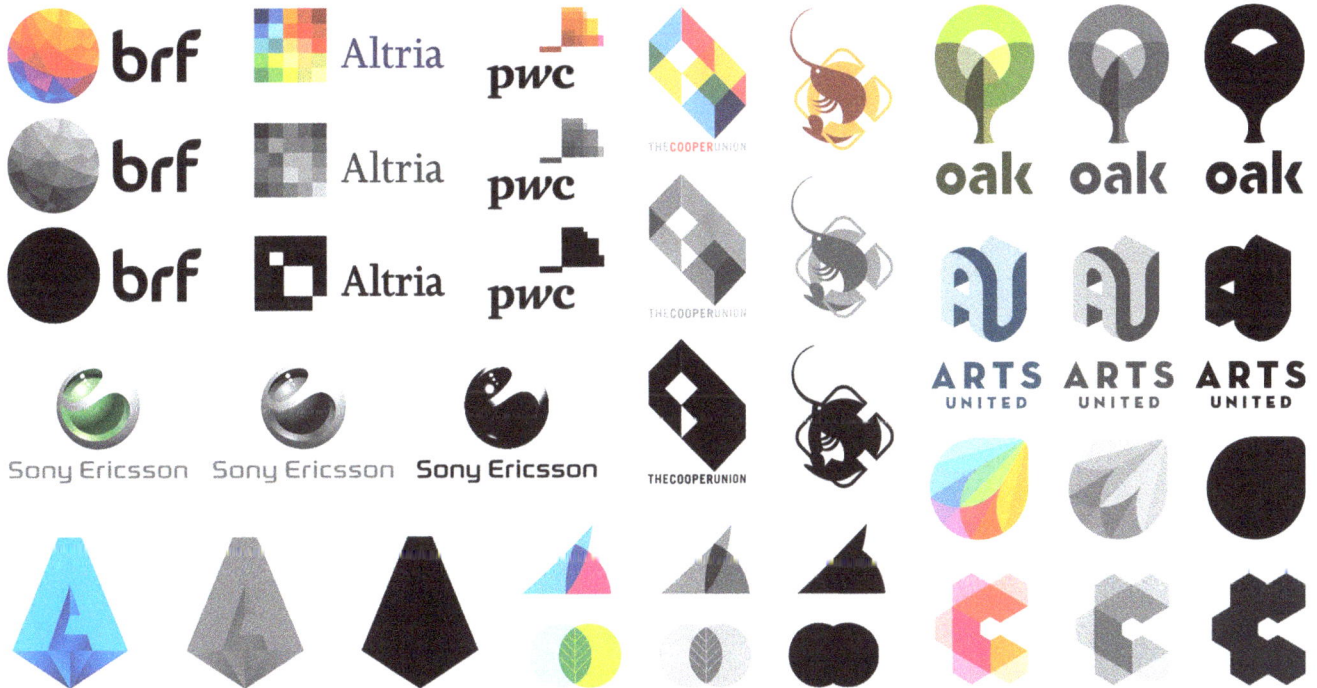

Losing the crutch of color, can these logos walk on their own? Some limp along; some fall flat. Unwary designers might look at these and say, "Wow! That's never been done before." They should stop and ask why. Maybe it's because it was a bad idea and previous designers understood the basic principles of identity design and wisely stayed away from such approaches.

Chapter 23

Deadly Sin of Logo Design #2:

Lack of Mass

Mass gives an identity visibility at a distance or in small sizes. The shapes that make up the identity should not be lightweight or thin. An identity with insubstantial and flimsy parts is ineffectual and visually feeble.

Some diehards will suggest that contemporary identities can break older rules in the name of being modern. Now I ask: aren't websites modern? The bottom-right corner of the illustration here shows lines that are supposed to be black, but are so thin that none of the pixels of the logo are a genuine black, nor even close to it. This is a problem I call "Pixel Mush." Thin elements and lines do not display clean shapes when viewed through a grid of pixels. Far from liberating lazy designers from old constraints, the Web adds new constraints of its own.

I propose a small experiment. For this, you will have to practice using what I call a "cold eye," which means to look at things as if you had never seen them before. Ask yourself, "If I did not already know what these images are, could I tell now?" That's using a cold eye.

Now look up a page in this book of logos by one of the great masters of design, Paul Rand or Saul Bass (Chapter 12). Or if those two are too historical for you, look up the logos of Chermayeff & Geismar & Haviv, whose company is still producing identities for major companies all around the globe. Stand back several feet. See how far you can go before being unable to discern the individual designs of the great logo designers. Then look at the logos below, at the same distance, and with a cold eye. Can you see the problem now? By comparison, they are barely discernible.

All of these suffer from lack of mass. The problem is compounded if mid- or light-mid value colors are used. The logo in the bottom-right corner has difficulty on the web because the lines are so thin they have to be made up of pixels that are not fully black, even though the line is supposed to be black. That's what I call "Pixel Mush."

One large and famous New York design studio has dozens of high-profile identity designs to its credit. Here is a black-and-white poster from the studio's own website that displays 458 logos. Many of them are good, serviceable identities. But notice how some are recessive and hard to discern because of lack of mass. This is particularly true of some of the typographic identities. If they don't have a certain minimum amount of mass, they are hard to see. They're wimpy.

I rest my case.

Please note that I did not alter this image. It is taken directly from the studio's own website, pixel-for-pixel, yet it demonstrates how breaking either of these two Deadly Sins is, indeed, fatal to producing a legible identity – even if you are a famous design studio.

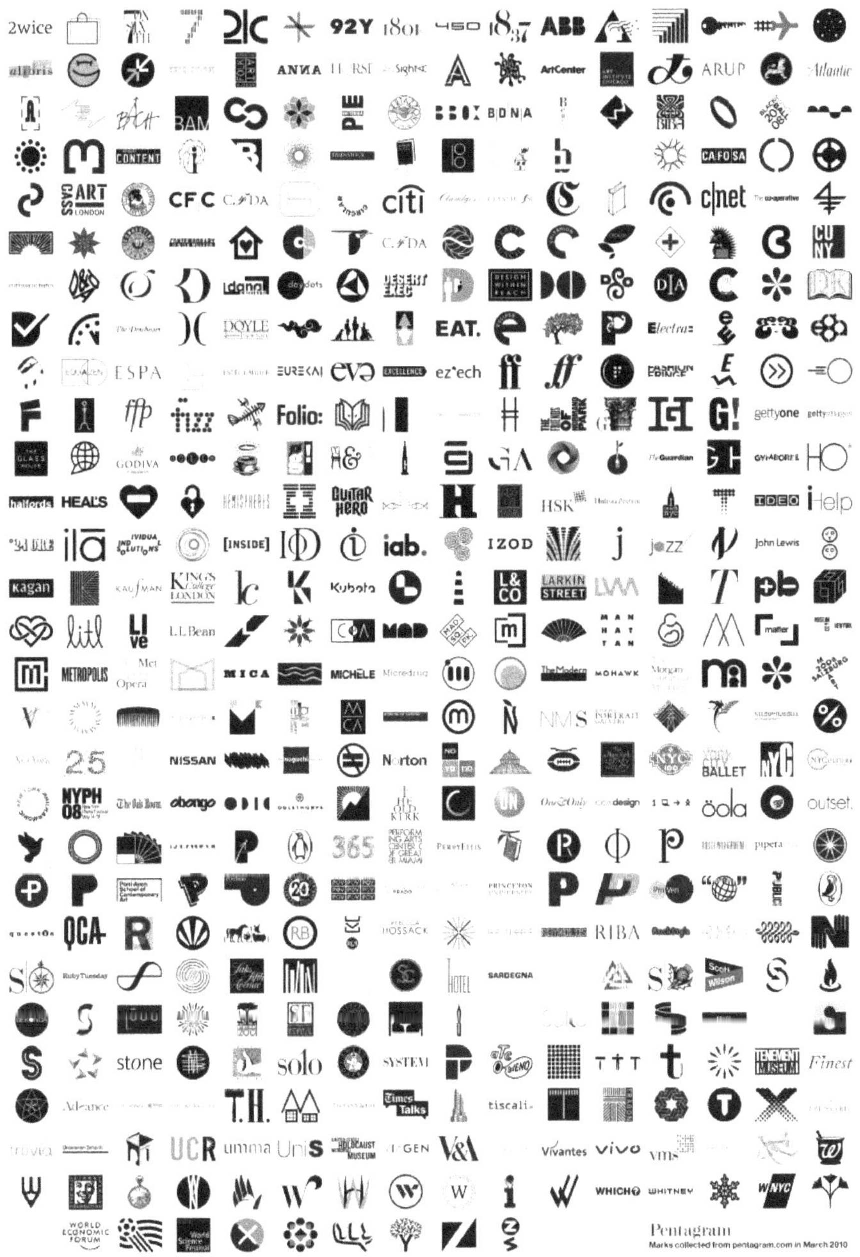

Shown here are 458 identities created by a famous design studio in New York. This image is pixel-for-pixel as it appeared on their own website. Note that many identities have no mass and consequently are hard or impossible to discern, while others that occupy the same space are very easy to make out..

Some may observe that images on the web at a nominal 72 pixels per inch will not convert to print, where 300 pixels per inch is the standard. True. Others may claim that the logos shown on the previous page are so small that it is unreasonable to expect them to be legible. But some of those logos do very well in spite of their small size while others are indistinct.

Even so, to allay any fears that I have cited a sample that doesn't properly apply, I also found on the same company's website many of the same logos and reproduced much larger. I show them here at a higher resolution. The principle still holds true: identities without mass do not project themselves as well as those with mass. Some don't show up for other reasons, such as failing to work in black only. And some have visual difficulties for reasons that will be covered in upcoming Deadly Sins.

This principle of needing mass also applies to the typographic elements of an identity, but we will come back to those issues later.

Two Deadly Sins down. Five to go.

Even with the same studio's logos shown bigger (in the order they appear on the website), those lacking mass, or that need multiple values (Deadly Sin #1), suffer from decreased legibility.

Chapter 24

Deadly Sin of Logo Design #3:

Obscure Contrast

Legibility is readability, the capacity to be correctly perceived or clearly deciphered. Legibility is a function of contrast. And contrast is a function of value. It doesn't matter so much what the hue or saturation is in the colors. What matters most for contrast is sufficient difference in value.

Any logo that has low contrast – and therefore low legibility – has failed its very reason for being: to be clearly seen and read.

There are two major kinds of contrast, and they are both essential for a good corporate identity: external contrast and internal contrast.

External contrast means having a good value difference between the design and the background. Internal contrast means that the logo elements can be distinguished from one another. A good identity has both.

This is another drawback to using gradients, photographs or illustrations as logos. In one area there may be sufficient contrast, but in others not.

One recurring pitfall that some designers fall into is trying to use all three of the primary colors in an identity. It *never* works. Yellow is a very light color, and consequently will not show up well against a white background.

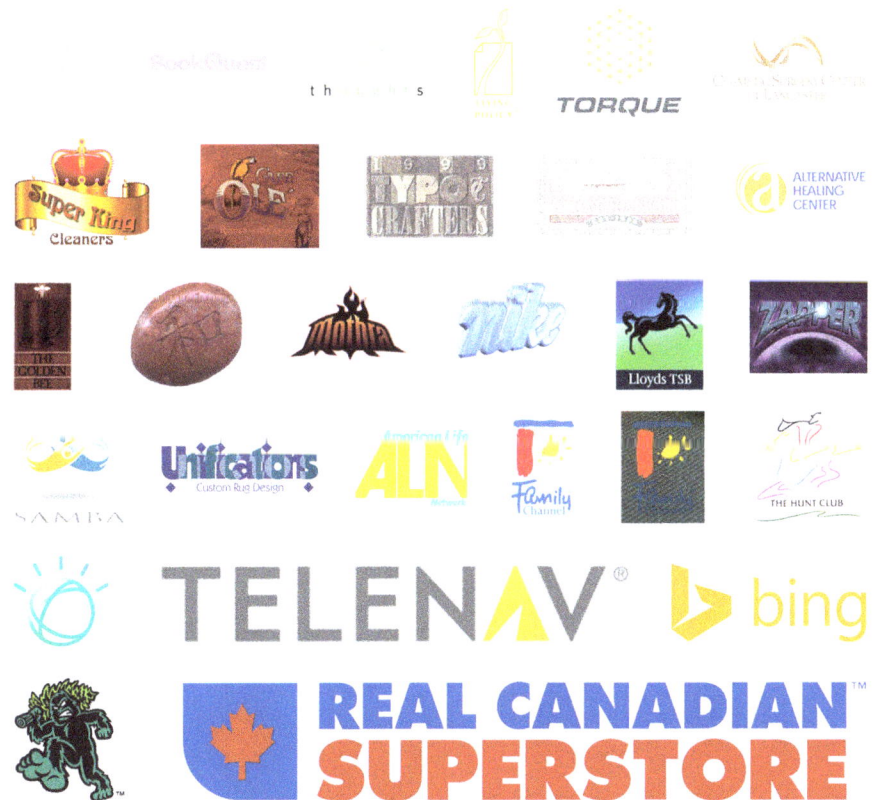

Some of these have poor contrast on a white background. Some have poor internal contrast. The old Family Channel logo had poor contrast on both light and dark backgrounds because the designer insisted on using the "primary colors."

Most shades of blue are too dark to show up against a dark background. Red is usually a mid-value color and will not show up against a mid-value background. Therefore, any identity that uses all three primary colors risks having some part fail to show up, no matter what value background is used. It is one of those "great ideas" that isn't great after all.

As we discussed before, it is helpful to think of the values of colors as percents. 100% as black; 0% as white, etc. Since a signature needs to be easily read to be effective, it needs to have 60% contrast or more with its background. A logo can have less contrast, as little as 40% with the background. But if a logo has multiple colors–not something that is recommended in the first place–then the elements inside need to have 30% or 40% contrast from each other to be effective. As you can see from the grayscale version of the samples from the previous page, every one of these fail completely at this.

A designer can sculpt the most exquisite shapes with the best proportions and then ruin the design by choosing colors that give poor contrast.

Sounds like a blowout, doesn't it?

This is a grayscale image of the examples from the previous page and is an accurate representation of the inherent value of all of those colors. The yellow used for the bing identity above is a 25% gray, too light for good legibility for a logo (40% or more), much less what is needed for an effective signature (60% or more). Golds and yellows are really only effective against dark backgrounds. On positive backgrounds an alternate color needs to be chosen.

Chapter 25

Deadly Sin of Logo Design #4:

Wayward Parts (Parts Out of Harmony)

Visual conflict – elements that don't harmonize—is another big pitfall in identity design. Because there are so many different manifestations of this particular deadly sin, we will look at numbered examples.

Slapping a shape on some letters without considering the relative contours is another all-too-common kind of lazy design **(1)**.

Sometimes elements are not compatible or are mismatched in some manner. Here **(5)** we have a baroque-style illustration (we already have identified illustrations as a problem) together with type from the 1960s and the '80s.

Another kind of disparity happens when designers try to create their own type **(4)**. Most designers do not have the typographic skill to pull this off, and the results will usually look amateurish.

Rarely does using a logo as the first letter in the signature work well **(7, 10, 11)**. It disrupts the easy reading of the

signature. It's even worse if the logo is used to replace some letter in the middle of a signature **(3, 6, 9)**. If the letter is the same size as the other letters but very different in design, there is a discontinuity in reading the signature, and the word seems split in two.

Treating letters in a single word in different graphic styles or colors **(8)** is also disruptive to reading the word. Is it two words or one? The same disruption happens when some letters are a different size. Generally, it is better to keep the logo separate from the signature **(6)**. Otherwise, just design a cohesive wordmark to begin with.

Yet a different kind of wayward design is when the mood or imagery are at odds with a professional image that befits the company. This can happen in many different ways but, often it is a question of the design shapes reminding the viewer of something not intended or promoting association with incompatible ideals.

1.

2.

3.

4.

5.

6.

7.

8.

9.

10.

11.

77

Specific note on #2: Are those people in silhouette or bird droppings? What company would want that association?

Finally, a design that shows a double-entendre is a serendipitous delight, but when two or more concepts are forced together poorly or in an overly contrived manner, the result is a disastrous hodgepodge **(3, 5, 7)**. This is akin to using every spice you have in a stew: garlic, cinnamon, thyme, peppermint and cayenne all together.

Chapter 26

Deadly Sin of Logo Design #5:

Overlapped Elements

Overlapping elements was once a popular technique in identity designs, but people learned more than a hundred years ago that it reduces legibility.

Placing type over an image makes both the image and the type harder to read. Similar to overlapping is the practice of placing the signature inside a visual element, which makes the type subordinate to the visual and reduces legibility. When the signature type is very brief, it can work, but only marginally. Larger signatures suffer considerably from this approach. It should be avoided.

Each of these companies learned for themselves that overlapped elements don't work well and have abandoned them. Type is either subordinated inside the logo or legibility is compromised—or both.

Putting type over any other element(s) ever helps legibility. Sometimes overlapping with lighter elements can be survived (1, 2, 4) but the text is *not* made easier to read by doing so. When the type over an element is only middle value (3), legibility is forfeited.

When any text is placed over a busy background, elements that are both light and dark, (5, 6, 7, 10, 11, 13) legibility is severely compromised. (see Busy Backgrounds in Chapter 8.)

Placing text inside another element makes it subordinate to the element, often making the text too small for clarity. For instance, in the Conte's identity (9), did you notice the words "MARKET & GRILL" in the upper fin and "WESTPORT" in the lower fin? Didn't think so.

Placing the logo in the middle of a two-word signature (14) disrupts the reading of the signature. Then, separating it from the signature for a different layout becomes a breach of design continuity. Best to not do it at all.

Even in a relatively clear logo like Best Buy (12), the words were always subordinated to the label shape. In its improved new design, the Best Buy label element is separated from the signature and the whole identity is cleaner.

Capital One (15), on the other hand, has fixed the word "One" that was in a low contrast gray, but improved nothing by adding a hackneyed swoosh shape that intersects the signature, making it harder to read.

Separating the Pepto-Bismol signature from the pink shape has lost nothing of esthetic importance (16).

1.

2.

3.

4.

5.

6.

7.

8.

9.
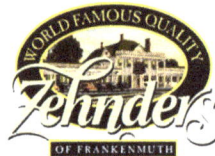
10.

11.
12.

13.

14.
15.
16.
17.

18.

19.

Often the motivation to overlap identity elements is little more than an attempt to camouflage uninspired, lackluster or mismatched elements (8, 17, 18). Happily, some clients have jettisoned their sub-par logos for new, cleaner ones without overlapping elements (16, 17, 18.) Arianespace's new logo is better designed and separating the elements improves legibility.

The Utah Jazz identity has taken a drastic turn for the worse by sacrificing clear and unified type for a sickly conceived and executed letter "J"

cobbled together from other poorly drawn parts. Furthermore, the secondary shadow line on the main letters compromises clarity, especially in front of the word UTAH, where it could be easily mistaken for an extra letter "I."

As with any other action that lessens clarity, overlapping elements should be avoided. It may not be a total disaster, but it *never* improves legibility. Instant clarity and readability are indispensable qualities of successful corporate identity.

Chapter 27

Deadly Sin of Logo Design #6:

Unrefined Shapes

Vector art is the medium in which all identities should be created, but it can be deceptive. It can give the impression that shapes are better than they are because the edges are crisp and clean without necessarily being well rendered or refined. This can be especially true when altering letterforms (2, 7) if the designer fails to be sensitive to the inherent shapes of the font. Something about Intel's logo must have bothered the company because they have replaced the design.

Lack of sensitivity to angles is another common shortcoming. In (4) the angles of the "f" are not the same as the angles of the containing box, neither coinciding nor contrasting. Irregular gaps between elements of (5) are laughable, not to mention the clumsy treatment of the letters themselves. And speaking of poorly rendered letterforms, (12) is obviously not a properly rendered type font design.

Curves also demand sensitive execution. Initially they can look passable, but on further inspection, we notice that subtle sensitivities are missing. Over time, these clumsy curves become irksome and grating (3, 9, 10). With curves, our eyes are coaxed into following a particular sweep. If the trajectory deviates from the anticipated course, it is disruptive. If it is overt and explicit, it becomes a focal point. If it is merely an unskilled deviation, it is a mark of amateur drawing. Note the inept curves in (9) and how curves are not even attempted in the bottoms of the sails.

Here we come to a principle I call Visual Logic. Everything you draw sets up a visual expectation for the rest. In a series of uniform structures, one element that is slightly atypical will stick out like the proverbial sore thumb. If the difference is deliberate, overt and skillfully done, it becomes a point of emphasis. If it is not, it just comes across as ineptitude and clumsiness. In (11) the thickness of the straight lines is close, but not the same as those of the containing circle, and for no good reason. In (8) the lines converge to form a solid, but the perimeter of that convergence edge is lumpy and uneven.

Interestingly, when designers reach too far, they can over-stylize or over-refine an identity to the point of making it unrecognizable. Prudential Life insurance (6) had this happen when they simplified their logo so much that people no longer perceived the Rock.

IBSEN 2006

1.   2.   3.   4.   5.

6.   7.   8.   9.

OUELLET

10.   11.   12.

DYNASTAR

of Gibraltar. They had to back off to a stylized but identifiable graphic.

Likewise, the designers of the Ibsen wordmark took their quest for "leading edge" to such an extent that they hoped people would read a lower-case "I" from a mere dot (1). It is too much to expect.

Spotify has a logo that looks like concentric arcs on first glance. But on closer examination, it is clumsy in the extreme. Spotify made a change in its identity recently, but has not gotten around to fixing their bungled logo.

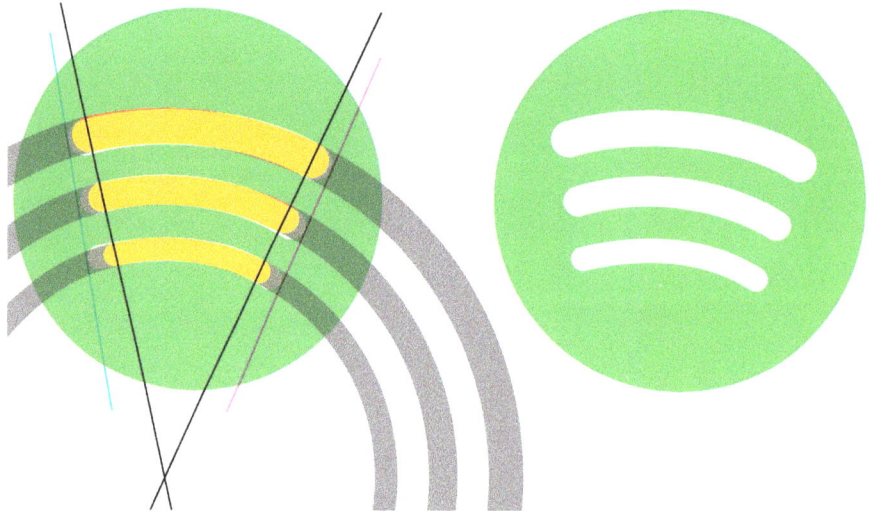

One of the leading music streaming apps is Spotify. That makes it a technology company. One might expect exactness in a logo for that kind of company. How sad that they have such an unrefined logo. One may look at the concentric arcs and think there's something a bit off. But when overlaid with geometrically drawn concentric arcs, one can really see what a slipshod job they have done with their logo. They've only been around since 2008 and have updated their identity two times since then, but never bothered fixing the sloppy arcs in their logo.

Chapter 28

Deadly Sin of Logo Design #7:

Tiny Elements, Thin Lines

We have already dealt with the problem of overall mass. A similar but distinct issue is that of tiny elements or thin lines, even when found in a logo that has sufficient overall mass.

In every kind of printing, be it offset, letterpress, laser or ink jet, there is a similar drawback. I call it Ink Creep: the ink from the bigger object fills in fine negative lines to some degree. If the lines are substantial enough, the line survives this minute encroachment. On the other hand, if the gap is thin, it can fill in or at least be compromised. This is why experienced designers don't use type with small serifs in reverse: the serifs fill in. Fine reversed lines in a logo are subject to a similar fate. Of course, thin positive lines in a logo become thin negative lines when the logo is reversed.

This problem is not eliminated in the digital world. We view all digital media through a grid of pixels. Admittedly, the grids are getting finer as screen resolutions for electronic devices go up. Regardless, Pixel Mush reasserts itself. To review, Pixel Mush happens when shapes or lines are so small that they cannot be rendered with either a pixel in the solid identity color or solid background color. If the identity colors are black and white, edges will be anti-aliased, which means that gray pixels are used on the edge to disguise the pixel grid. Anti-aliasing gives a smoother edge to elements on the screen and hides the "jaggies." But this useful technological visual help is a double-edged sword. In a black logo on a white background, very thin white lines may be rendered only in gray because the lines aren't wide enough for any pixels to be completely white or black. In a series of thin lines or gaps, lines can appear darker or lighter due to the number of pixels that make them up respectively.

This principle applies to typography as well, and is why fonts in the Didone family (such as Bodoni, Modern, Didot, etc.) are so seldom used in identity design. They have some nice, thick strokes, but they also have very thin strokes that tend to disappear, especially when the type is reversed.

Some came from glossy magazines, with printing as good as one can expect, and yet, the logos have filled in. The fault is not in the printing but in the designs. Other samples were taken directly from vector files, as accurate as digital files can be. But images get translated into pixels. This book uses 300 pixel per inch. Even so, lines that should be uniform appear varied and groups of lines which should be the same appear to get lighter and darker. Pixels are a fact of life, especially on the web. Lines or gaps too small always cause problems.

Of all the Seven Deadly Sins, using elements too small or lines too thin is perhaps the most common, second only to designing a logo that fails to work in solid black.

The "too small, too thin" sin is one of the few ever committed by great identity designers such as Paul Rand, Saul Bass or Chermayeff & Geismar & Haviv. In virtually every case where they used tiny elements or thin lines, the identities have been replaced or amended. Over the years, countless designers for many companies have produced logos with lines that are too thin for good, solid reproduction. Most of these companies have redesigned their logos to correct this. Rand and Bass even corrected this mistake in their own logos, IBM and AT&T respectively. They realized that you can't fight thin lines; you just have to get rid of them.

Some designers try to hide from this reality by specifying that their identity ought not be used below a certain size. Unfortunately, many times identities must be used smaller than the "allowable" minimum. Companies often work with other companies where the identities of all participants will be shown in a "logo soup." The costs of newspaper ads and Yellow Pages ads often encourage the use of smaller identities. But the coarser paper used in both of these further aggravates the effects of tiny elements and thin lines.

A related problem happens when any line tapers gradually to a fine point. Whenever these lines are reversed, ink fill-in will cut off the tip of the point. This may be why Facebook Messenger's icon has recently changed to have the two lines end with rounded points.

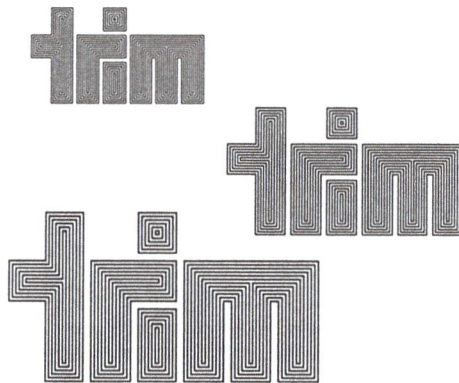

Sooner or later any identity will be used in reverse, so this principle applies to either positive or negative lines in any design. This is also why

fonts with fine lines are problematic for identities; the fine lines tend to suffer in positive and fill in when in reverse.

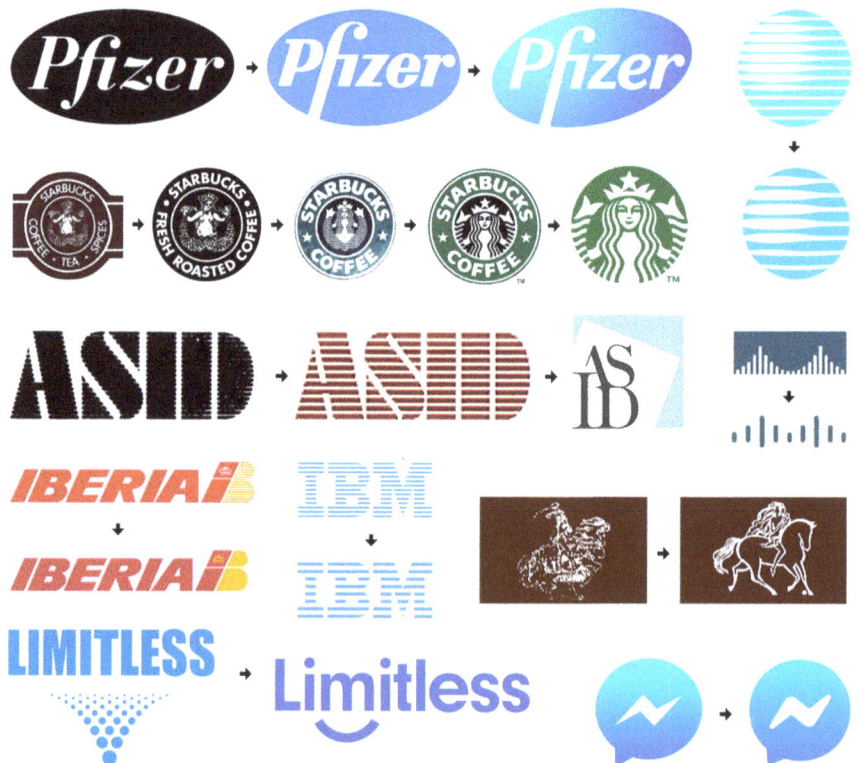

Each of these identities had lines or elements that were too fine and consequently did not reproduce at small or even reasonable sizes. In each case, the logos have been redesigned.

(Special note: Paul Rand recognized this problem in his first IBM logo and fixed it. Similarly, Saul Bass fixed this in his AT&T logo.)

Chapter 29

If You Take Away All the Seven Deadly Sins of Logo Design,

What's Left?

To recap the Seven Deadly Sins of Logo Design, they are:

B Can't work in solid **B**lack
L **L**ack of mass
O **O**bscure contrast
W **W**ayward or disharmonious parts
O **O**verlapped elements
U **U**nrefined shapes
T **T**hin lines, **T**iny elements

Some may not like them, but acronyms like BLOWOUT help me remember lists. I hope this works for you too.

Some designers may be dismayed by this list and say, "If you take away all the approaches that cause a BLOWOUT, there's so little left. How can we work?"

Remember: the essential quality of any good identity is instant recognition and clarity. Anything that detracts from that is counterproductive and contrary to what a good identity should be.

Others may be tempted to think, "All of the good designs have already been created using traditional methods. We have to go beyond them to find new and uncharted territory."

Still others may feel the old methods are too confining, too old-fashioned, too "been there, done that." They may think that for a truly contemporary identity, one should use new visual techniques—even if they don't really work.

Let's compare our visual world to the world of music. In Western culture, the ancient Greeks worked out for us the diatonic scale of notes. From the simple octave with its twelve possible notes, no end of music has been composed, century after century, style after style. Notwithstanding the invention of new musical instruments, modern composers

J. S. Bach - Beginning of the Prelude from the Suite for Lute in G minor

do not *require* new instruments to compose contemporary music.

If you were to hear on CNN, "Today the leading musicians of the world have agreed that no more good music can be composed; it's all been created," you might want to check to see if it's April Fool's Day.

All of the music that is possible from the same simple notes has not yet been written, nor will we *ever* reach a point where no new music can be created. In our analogy, new instruments could correspond to new visual media. Why would anyone say, then, that our creativity as designers is being stifled by the need to use the same basic principles of visual clarity that have been honed and refined over the long history of corporate identities?

Take heart. There will never be an end of good, well designed identities that work. Unfortunately, there will also be no end of poorly designed identities by people who have not learned the principles of this craft.

One need only look through design annuals to be inspired by new and marvelous design solutions for corporate identities. Sad to say, many of the bad examples shown in previous chapters were also published in these same design annuals. Publishing a design in a magazine and saying it is good doesn't make it good.

Remember: the purpose of a corporate identity is to clearly and instantly identify a company. Any factor that prevents that recognition is like the single hole in a balloon or a tire; it will cause a blowout.

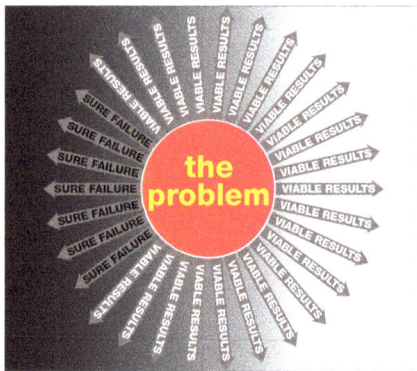

Why would anyone object to being warned about directions that guarantee failure? How can that stiffle creativity?

But it is not enough to know what to avoid in the Seven Deadly Sins of Logo Design. This book is not just about what not to do; it is also about how to design the right way.

So If we go back to our exploration of the three identity components (wordmarks, logos and monograms), and we've had a good self-brainstorming session (or better yet, multiple sessions) to come up with some ideas with each of the four possible concepts (corporate activity, corporate ideals, corporate name and abstract), we still have to decide how we are going to model, render or draw our identity.

Does the way you work affect the way you think? (the answer is yes!) "Wrench Hands, Nut Head" by A. Michael Shumate, 1990

After Brainstorming

After using the conceptualizing techniques discussed previously, a designer will have a number of possible concepts for any given identity project. Naturally, many concepts will be rather raw. Even so, looking at the shapes made for each concept may provide some opportunities for cross-fertilizing ideas.

The shapes in one concept may be just what another concept needs to make it work. This may foster a new round of conceptualizing based on the first round. As mentioned before, this process is best done manually with pencil in hand, not on the computer. Go to the computer vector program only for the final rendering.

After this stage, it may be necessary to visually process one or more concepts. A number of techniques can transform elements into something unique and useful. The same concept can be rendered using any number of beautiful techniques to give very different final results.

Visual Processing Techniques

Now let's look at some good visual approaches for executing a concept. Let's say you have decided on a lion as an appropriate concept for your client's logo. (Or an eagle, or a tree.) Any of those words may seem lame or over-used. Yes, there have been a million lion logos already, and maybe even half of them are good. That doesn't mean there can't be another good lion logo that is different from any lion logo that's ever been produced.

We've seen how you can kick-start your creative juices by pairing the three possible identity components with the four possible identity concepts. Similarly, you can develop a distinctive and esthetic mark through any of the main kinds of visual processing. I've identified ten of them. There may be more, and I'd love to hear from you if you know of another one. (We'll see them in the next section.)

To help with that process, I've developed another acronym: CPFULLNESS. It can stand for Creative Priming FULLNESS or Cool Potential FULLNESS, or maybe even ConcePT FULLNESS. (Yeah, I know that acronyms, by their very nature, can be a bit contrived. But they can be helpful, too.)

Next we'll examine some great examples of visual techniques.

Section Five

Core Principles

Visual
Techniques

Any given concept
can be executed in virtually endless ways.
These techniques can transform a common concept
into an uncommon,
or even remarkable final identity.

Chapter 30

Logo Design Visual Technique #1:

Containment

I see Containment in two ways: Shallow Containment and Deep Containment.

Shallow Containment

This is merely placing a shape around a signature. Consequently, the image has not much more design value added than a plain signature. As I said before, a signature alone (merely choosing a certain font to write the company's name) gives little value added and is mostly reserved for consumer product identities and the companies that make them. It is less well suited to other kinds of corporate identities.

Some uninspired designers will also add a shape to a poorly conceived or executed logo to mask its deficiencies. Again, Shallow Containment. It is an unfortunately common practice.

Shallow Containment: Placing a shape around a signature (which is mostly just selecting a font to write the company name). As with un-contained signatures, this technique is used mostly for consumer products and is not as suitable for other kinds of corporate identities.

Deep Containment

On the other hand, the use of a containing shape can sometimes be the salvation of a decent design that might fail due to other considerations, such as lack of contrast (16). In sample (1), for instance, the leading edge of a white golf ball would have no contrast against a white background. The addition of "zoom marks" on the dark side completes the edge.

Containing a design can give a logical boundary or stopping place for an image, like a picture frame (2, 8, 12, 23).

Containers can contribute mass to designs that might be too insubstantial without them (2, 4, 6, 17, 20, 21). Containers can compensate somewhat for a color that is almost too light (14, 22), giving the design color mass, distinct from image mass already mentioned.

Containers can provide unity and cohesiveness to word-cluster-style wordmarks or reinforce the shapes in a wordmark (7, 9, 13).

Containment can echo the shape of a specific letterform (17, 18, 19, 22). Containers can contrast with the shapes contained (3, 5, 6, 12, 15, 20) or harmonize with them (7, 11, 14, 17, 18, 19). Containment can give symmetry or help center unsymmetrical shapes (3, 5, 8, 12, 14, 15, 20). Containment can change the overall shape of the significant design element (3, 6, 10, 12, 15, 20, 22).

Containment can be the template for the whole design (11, 19).

Meaningful containment is a useful visual treatment and should be part of every identity designer's tool box.

1.   2.   3.   4.   5.   6.

7.   8.   9.   10.   11.

12.   13.   14.   15.   16.   17.

18.   19.   20.   21.   22.   23.

Chapter 31

Logo Design Visual Technique #2:

Planar or Silhouette

A planar image is one that renders shadows as a solid dark color, and lighter parts as a solid light color or white, with no shading (1-10). A silhouette is similar but uses only the contour of the whole subject and disregards any light falling on it (11-20).

Both of these are common techniques for making logos with strong imagery in solid colors. Most of the samples are photographically realistic drawings; however, some (8, 10, 14, 20) use a non-realistic style.

Even though some of these designs use more than one color (3, 6, 7, 8 17, 18), the secondary colors could be printed in white or black.

A separate consideration from the overall drawing style (realistic or non-realistic) is the edge quality. This can add distinct flavor without changing the drawing style. Notice how the edges of each shape can be rectilinear -- (all of 2), or (just the face 6). On the other hand, all edges can be made curvilinear with either an s-curve or graceful arc (4, 11) and just the cloak (6).

Planar and silhouette renderings can also use other systems of shapes. For instance, (14) is an interesting combination of almost geometric curves with straight lines. The gold halo used on (18) can easily be omitted in one-color situations.

Top half: Logos using planar shapes to represent three-dimensional images by using solid colors. Bottom half: Logos using silhouettes either as positive images or reversed out of a solid containment shape or another element.

The same image can be realistically drawn but have a "flavor"
added to it by the kind of edge line
used to render it. Here we can see
the flavors of edge line quality and
its contribution to the end image.
First we see a realistic rendering
with natural edge line quality.

Second is a rectilinear rendering;
notice that each shape is reproduced more or less accurately but
only with straight edges lines.

Next we see the same shapes with
a curvilinear flavor; each edge line
is either an s-curve or a graceful
arc. Note that different joining
lines meet at sharp corners. This
accentuates the curves. If the lines
had met with rounded corners, the
effect would have been blobby and
the lines would have seemed less
elegant. These edge line quality
flavors can be used on planar images as in this sample, or on silhouettes.

Separate from the edge line quality
can be the overall drawing style.
The overall style of the first three
samples was realistic, the image
above has been distorted.

Chapter 32

Logo Design Visual Technique #3:
Fragmentation

A design can be broken up into smaller portions using stripes, dots, triangles or any other repeatable solid shape. These shapes can be tapered (in the case of lines) or rendered at different sizes (in the case of dots, triangles or squares). Grids can be employed to keep the units even or progressively larger and smaller. Vector programs like Adobe Illustrator can be useful in creating such fragmentations.

Fragmentation can provide some of the benefits of gradients without the shortcomings. It can also give the illusion of different values while using one solid color, again, without any of its drawbacks.

When using fragmentation, avoid making any sub-shapes too small. Otherwise, you fall into the pit of Tiny Elements and Thin Lines (Deadly Sin of Logo Design #7). Rather than using twelve lines to fragment an element, try eight or seven. This is the very lesson that Paul Rand learned with his own IBM logo and Saul Bass with his AT&T logo (see Chapter 28).

When using tapering lines, it is important to avoid making the ends with too fine a tapering point. Such needle-like points can be subject to filling in or dropping off. Either make tapering lines with blunt tips or increase the angle of taper at the ends to make pointss that are less visually fragile. The value of doing this may not be apparent with a positive version, but every logo ought to be able to be reversed. Printing any fragmented design in reverse may show fine points that are in danger of filling in.

When in doubt, try a test print of the logo design in positive, and reverse at only a half-inch high—or even smaller—on regular or even poor quality paper. Is the print clear? Do the fragmentations remain separate and clean? If not, try fewer and larger fragmentations.

Recently there have been numerous logos designed that are made of many colorful facets. Some of them are beautiful. But they are also fatally flawed because they typically do not reproduce well in grayscale, having poor internal

As long as care has been taken to avoid Deadly Sin of Logo Design #7 (Tiny Elements or Thin Lines), fragmentation can be effective.

contrast, and do not keep their faceted quality when rendered as solid black.

With some of these identities, the designers have seen the deficiencies and have designed an alternate design for one-color usage with separated facets. But this means that the one-color version is actually a different design, underscoring the original design's flaws.

The solution is simple. Just separate the facets into discrete parts with a gap between each element in the first place. This prevents having two designs: a separated and non-separated one, which are really two different designs. Here care must be taken so that gaps are not too small, but this approach can work for a cleaner multi-color version, grayscale and in solid black.

Here are two samples of a common variety of very colorful logos being created lately (A). However, these often do not convert well to grayscale (B) and lose their multi-faceted quality altogether in one solid color (C).

The solution is to fragment the facets to begin with (D). This may inspire an overall simplification, (not a bad thing), but the result will hold together better as both grayscale (E) and in any solid color (F).

Three Fortune 500 Companies, Leidos, Assurant and American Tower respectively, have multicolored logos (A). The first two also have black & white versions with altered logos (B). This logo design change has a different feeling apart from the lack of colors. A better solution is to design both the color and B&W versions with separated elements (C). This gives better clarity in color versions and keeps the logo designs identical.

Chapter 33

Logo Design Visual Technique #4:
Unique Coincidence

Every new client's corporate activity, ideals, name or initials carry unique visual opportunities that will work only for that particular kind of business or name or set of letters.

When conceptualizing, take some time to play with the letters or images involved. Imagine images upside down. Try them in mirror image. Look at the sketches you are considering. Are there shapes that can work well together? Explore different fonts and ways of making letters. Pay attention to overall shapes, to the negative spaces, to possible ways of joining shapes. Strip away preconceptions; let the edges blur in your mind. You are less likely to see unique coincidences at first glance when you are thinking too literally, or if you're working on a computer, they present themselves more often with paper and pencil.

These kinds of serendipitous joinings most often percolate to the top when you have time to fiddle with the bits and let the magic happen. Such coincidences can't be forced, but when they work well, they are a joy to see.

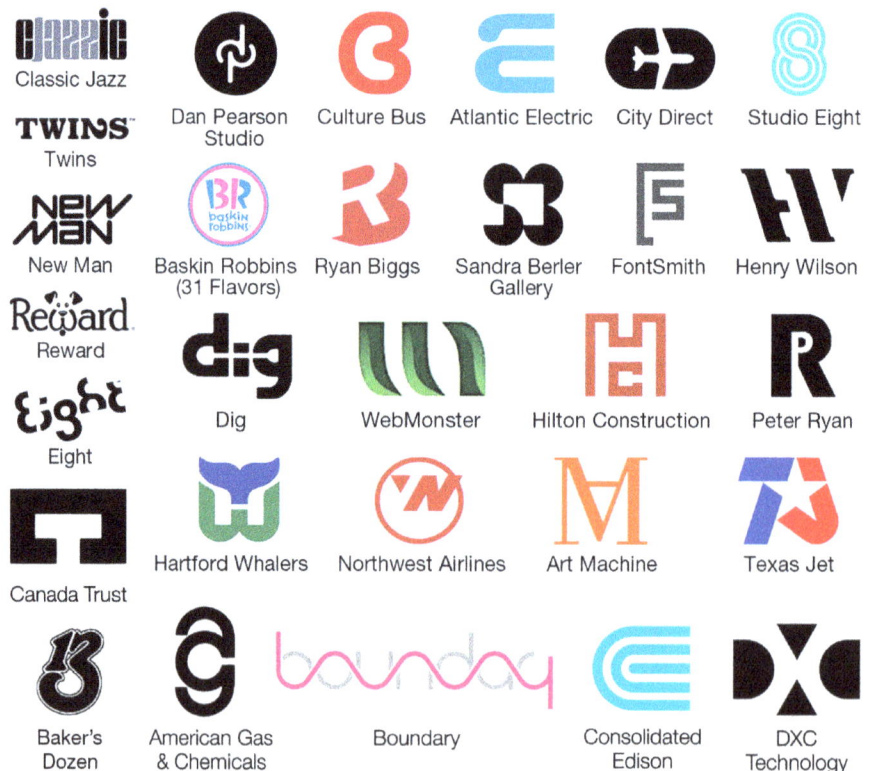

Classic Jazz

Twins

New Man

Reward

Eight

Canada Trust

Dan Pearson Studio

Culture Bus

Atlantic Electric

City Direct

Studio Eight

Baskin Robbins (31 Flavors)

Ryan Biggs

Sandra Berler Gallery

FontSmith

Henry Wilson

Dig

WebMonster

Hilton Construction

Peter Ryan

Hartford Whalers

Northwest Airlines

Art Machine

Texas Jet

Baker's Dozen

American Gas & Chemicals

Boundary

Consolidated Edison

DXC Technology

Each of these concepts is unique to the particular letters used in combination with the corporate name, activity, ideals or fonts being experimented with. If that experimentation had not happened, these delightful identities would never have been created.

Chapter 34

Logo Design Visual Technique #5:

Linear Treatment

As with fragmentation, the technique of rendering the whole identity with lines alone risks making the lines or spaces too delicate for clarity in small sizes or viewed from a distance. Drawing lines that are too lightweight for the overall size will make the whole logo too insubstantial (Deadly Sin of Logo Design #2: Lack of Mass). If lines are close together, it is safest to make lines and gaps the same thickness.

Why?

Because sooner or later, gaps become positive lines and lines become gaps when the identity is reversed.

Most of the samples shown here have decent mass. When designing with this technique, a good test is to print a design at no bigger than one-half inch on plain paper. If it is indistinct or begins to blur or fill in, either the rendering needs to be simplified or the lines (or gaps between) need increased weight.

A good rule of thumb is: make all lines either of uniform thickness or of variable thickness. Don't mix techniques (remember: coincide or contrast). Tools like Adobe Illustrator are particularly good at keeping strokes exactly the same and separating one stroke from another at exact distances. Line end caps and corners can be blunt, mitered or round.

Generally speaking, fewer lines are better than many, and heavier lines are better than fine. Some of these could be stronger by taking that advice.

We now can make vector strokes of variable thickness. Here again, strive for the beauty and grace of simplicity. Bezier curved lines are inherently more graceful when the fewest possible anchor points are used. The same is true of making lines thick and thin: the fewest changes will give the most graceful lines. Even lines that just taper at the ends, and are mostly of uniform thickness otherwise, can be effective.

Another consideration is how lines join at corners. If they join with sharp points, that can accentuate the curvilinear quality of the line. Ironically, lines joined in rounded corners will just look blobby and will not produce as curvaceous an effect.

The secret to elegant thick and thin lines is to only have one thick spot per line segment (between corners). You can go thin-to-thick-to-thin or you can go just thin-to-thick.

Chapter 35

Logo Design Visual Technique #6:

Ligatures, Swashes and Flourishes

Ligatures and flourishes (or swashes) will be useful mostly as options for wordmarks and monograms because they are typographic in nature. Indeed, employing either can change an ordinary signature into a wordmark.

Ligature pairs for certain letter combinations were part of moveable type from the very beginning of printing.

Ligatures

Typographic ligatures have existed from the first days when moveable type was invented, carrying over many of the handwriting conventions of the times into the new medium of printing. Letters in the words "The," "Of" and "And" were often combined into single ligatures, and dozens of other letter combinations were among the first sets of lead type ever cast. However, as many new fonts were not designed with ligature variants, the use of ligatures declined by the first half of the 20th century.

Here are some of Herb Lubalin's ligatures in his Avant Garde font. Although ligatures were originally unique joinings of adjacent letters, the term now could apply to any alternative letterform variation or interaction between letters.

GE VAIO ESPN cotton

Cadbury trafiq SanDisk®

Pinterest STAR WARS VOYAGE

Exxon KONTRAST rambla

ADP® UHS PACCAR

Flourishes and Swashes

Another typographic variation that goes well with ligatures is the making of decorative additions such as swashes or flourishes.

Some of these typographic deviations can communicate either an antique or a modern quality. Flourishes and swashes can imply fun and recreation and are consequently popular in certain segments of identity design, such as the food and drink industry, restaurants and rock bands.

Again, the key rule is: do not impede legibility by obscuring letterforms. It is one thing to use convoluted type on a magazine article title, where it can be an entertaining puzzle. That doesn't work for wordmarks for corporate identities. The whole raison d'être of an identity is to be instantly and easily recognized.

Ligatures can be old-fashioned or modern.

ANGELICA KITCHEN StoneBolt 1. Les Petit Café Smoothies BLAST MANGO The HOURGLASS HIBISCUS TeaLounge 2. 2. OLD CROW GAZETTE Fritos BRAND LoneStar De Rosa's BRICK OVEN PIZZA AT THE FIREHOUSE Calligraffiti 3. Falstaff 4. Passion Projects 5. Kate Murphy Photography 5. Stove Top

1. Tom Nikosey, 2. Michael Manoogian, 3. Niels Shoe Meulman, 4. David Quay, 5. Jessica Hische, all others: unknown.

1. The Barley Top Shop
2. Barista Fine Coffee Purveyors
3. Saffire
4. Renaissance Raven
5. Lisbon Lovers
6.
7. The Soulless
8.
9. Cedar House Soaps — Handcrafted Quality — Since 1000
10. Seasons Café — Salida Colorado
11. Biltmore — Asheville North Carolina — Est. 1895

Designing a corporate identity that has to be deciphered, unraveled or decoded is not a viable option. It goes against the very purpose of an identity: to easily identify the party in question. When it comes to people easily reading what you've created, you don't get three strikes; it's one strike and you're out. Sometimes designers get so fixated on typographic creativity that they don't realize that their decorations are conflicting with the letterforms, or that the design contains other visual conflicts like poor contrast or busy backgrounds.

When used well, ligatures, swashes and flourishes are powerful tools that can contribute to memorable designs with strong and unique visual entertainment value.

The important rule here is to avoid letting decorations either upstage the core letterforms of words embellished (3, 6) or interfere with them (2). This is easier to accomplish if you keep the decoration(s) outside the core of the letterforms. Sometimes decent typographic designs are undone by unnecessarily complicating the design with offset strokes (1) or textured backgrounds (6). Sometimes a fine design is undermined by contrasting the drop shadow with the background, and not the actual letterforms, (4). Sometimes letterforms are so stylized that people have difficulty reading the message, a consideration separate from the swashes or flourishes used (5, 8). The base letters are just too overwrought to be readable. The sad thing is that one doesn't have to sacrifice beauty for legibility as we see in (7 designed by David Ariail, 9 by Tobias Saul, 10 by Jared Jacob, 11 by Dave Stevenson).

Swashes are most successful when the core letterforms are not compromised.

Chapter 36

Logo Design Visual Technique #7:

Negative Shapes

Most letters have negative shapes or counters in them. They are more malleable and forgiving than the positive parts of letterforms and provide chances to create a double entendre while leaving the core letterform recognizable and readable. Many other images also can have both positive and negative shapes, such as those you might develop using the four conceptual approaches (Section 3). Why not combine the techniques? See what the counters of the letters remind you of. Look at the elements you associate with the company activity, ideals or name. Those concepts, too, may have negative shapes. You need to be open to a certain amount of visionary frolicking to let these ideas emerge

(that's why you should not conceptualize on the computer). In the end, it doesn't matter whether you consider the result a Negative Shape or a Unique Coincidence (Visual Technique #4), as long as you find the potential magic.

Here is where broad logo concept exploration bears fruit from earlier self-brainstorming. This is also where you will see the value of not editing during your concept generation, but rather, jotting down all the concepts that come to mind. When you combine a negative shape with a solid shape, a concept that might have looked lightweight, trite or even cheesy at the early stages can turn into a stroke of genius.

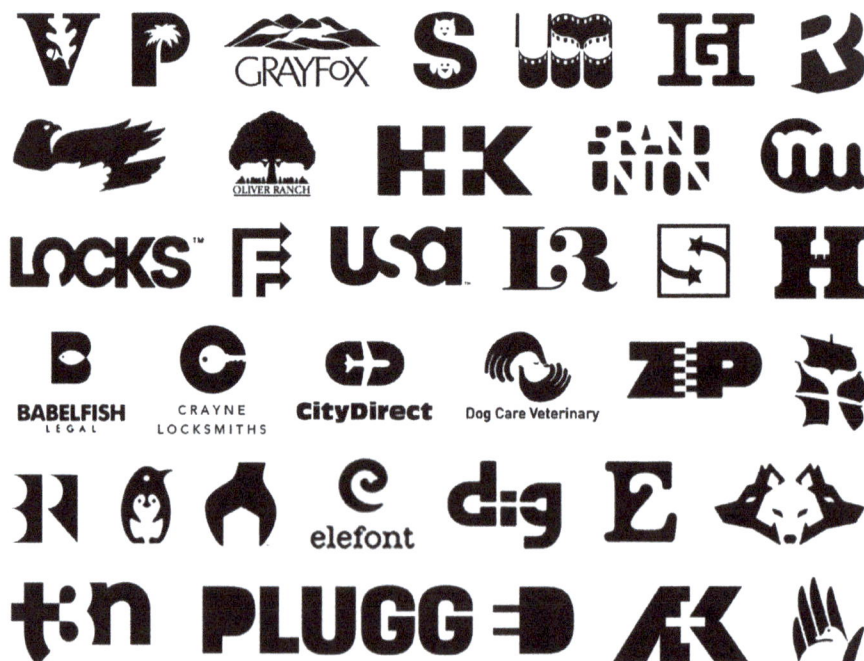

Negative shapes allow a visual double entendre. If you were working with only the positive shapes, it could look too contrived, forced or just unclear.

Chapter 37

Logo Design Visual Technique #8:

Essence

In identity design the most important question to ask is not "What can I add to this design?" but rather, "What can I remove? How can I simplify it, reduce it?" and "How can I show the essence of this subject?"

As we have stressed before, a good logo is not an illustration or a photograph. It is a symbol that reminds us of something, but it needs to be elegant in its restraint. This has been the whole trend of the corporate identity design industry for the past century (see Section 2).

Simplicity is the soul of good design, and it is the key to identities that stand the test of time. Pare down, simplify and find the essence of the image. This is where you can make your design exquisite – before you add colors or any other bells and whistles. Make a solid foundation, and you can build a solid identity. Skimp on this stage, and you will have made yet another mediocre logo that eventually will be replaced.

Of all the ten Visual Processing Techniques, striving for simplicity is one that should *always* be employed. Paradoxically, less detail and a cleaner rendering can mean a clearer image, which is the quality that the longest lasting identities share in common.

In the upper left is the old logo for Rockport Publishers and its newer replacement. See how the pared down, simpler logo is visually stronger and easier to read? Each other section shows logos not from the same company, but using the same visual subject. In each case, the first samples are more literal on the left and simpler on the right. Notice how each of the simpler logos is stronger, can be seen and comprehended more easily and will be more memorable than the more detailed and realistic versions.

Chapter 38

Logo Design Visual Technique #9:

A System of Shapes

The concept "system of shapes" may sound too formal and even a bit daunting to digest, but it is just a way of saying that any design can contain simple, repeated visual elements.

Finding the subject for the logo is just the beginning. Even with the simplest concepts, such as a single-letter monogram, there is virtually no end to ways of drawing it—or any other subject.

When using a system of shapes, one can impose a grid to reconstruct the image. Grids are handy for seeing relationships, measurements and angles. The grid can employ curved corners or not. Sometimes a particular curve or shape can be repeated to good effect. Those shapes could even come from the type font of the accompanying signature. Systems of shapes can be stylized, curvilinear, rectilinear, distorted, geometric or blended into some unique overall confining shape. The possibilities are endless, and surprisingly simple once you dissect them. As you begin to look for them, you will see all sorts of different visual systems for making logos. It can be helpful to collect them for future reference.

One easy method for getting the hang of this technique is to look at an existing logo. To avoid plagiarism, don't use the same subject; just copy the style or the system it uses. Now construct your image using that style or system of shapes. *Voilà!* A new and unique design.

Making a unique mark from an ordinary letter or subject is not hard. Here we have some Ws, trees, lions, stars, hearts and hands, and owls. Each logo is different from others of the same subject because each was constructed with its own system of shapes. You could make a new tree by using the system of shapes from one of the lions or a new W from the system of shapes from an owl. The possibilities are endless.

Make an A from the system of shapes used by the P, or a new B with the shapes from the S and you have a new design without plagiarism.

Here are 40 different eagle logo designs. Each uses repeated shapes, angles, line thicknesses. Some use geometric or other shapes to form parts. Each one is a system of shapes that could be used to draw a new logo. If the subject matter is different, you are not plagiarizing.

Each of these companies has a unique logo. They just all happen to be lions, but its the system of shapes that make each one unique.

Almost any concept for a logo probably has already been used. It is the visual treatment that distinguishes various logos. That often involves using a system of shapes as well as combining elements. Within a given logo, don't use more than one system of shapes.

103

Chapter 39

Logo Design Visual Technique #10:

Sculpted Type

Before the invention of moveable type, illustrated manuscripts featured hand-rendered lettering and embellished capitals. Hand typography was as free and as beautiful as its creators could make it. Although Gutenberg's invention allowed more books to be printed, type was limited to flat baselines with letters all the same height. Early on, drop caps and embellished capitals were developed for printing, but the baselines remained flat. Over the years, the appetite returned for customized, or, as I like to call it, "Sculpted Type," with non-linear baselines and flourishes.

Both Photoshop and Illustrator (and other similar software counterparts) have "Type Warp" tools for doing this. Unfortunately, these "Type Warp" tools do not respect individual letters, being only mathematical algorithms applied on whole words. The best practitioners of Sculpted Type tend to not use these tools, and I strongly recommend against them also. Instead, designers can achieve much better results by changing individual letters with the "shear" tool and fine-tuning letters by moving vector anchor points individually.

The beauty of what I call Sculpted Type (non-linear baselines), along with flourishes and swashes, is even more impressive when we consider that this typography was rendered by hand.

With the advent of the desktop computer, every designer has become a de facto typesetter, although with many of Gutenberg's original limitations. However, we now have digital tools for creating wordmarks with non-linear baselines that Gutenberg didn't have. With hand skills, even if digitally executed, one can produce excellent Sculpted Type for a wide variety of applications, including identities.

Note that with the exception of the Splayed Arc, the verticals in each letter remain vertical. Text Warp tools don't do that well in some of these configurations.

Flourishes and swashes (Visual Processing Technique #6) are frequent, welcome additions to Sculpted Type. This approach can be particularly effective in wordmark design to evoke associations with either old-fashioned nostalgia or futuristic mystique.

Great examples of Sculpted Type: 2, 3 Martin Schmetzer; 4 Mateusz Witczak; 5 Alan Ariail; 7, 8, 9 Tom Nikosey; 10 Dave Stevenson; 12 Audrey Ray; 14 Tobias Saul. 1, 11, 13 unknown.

Band identities do not have to sacrifice illegibility to be cool. Here are some decent examples. 5 Tom Nickosey, all others unknown.

Hand rendered titles from novels often employ sculpted type techniques. 1. Martin Schmetzer. All others unknown.

Sculpted Type is popular with several sectors of identity design. For instance, music bands—especially in the heavy-metal genre—often use sculpted type for their identities. Unfortunately, it is surprising how often legibility will be sacrificed for the perceived "cool factor" effect. Illustrated here are mostly legible samples. Others are nearly impossible to read. It almost seems as though the designs are manifesting the nihilist sentiments these groups seem to both espouse and engender, and are almost daring the reader to understand the wordmark. If so, they are defeating a wordmark's very purpose.

Certain segments of the book publishing industry, especially in the fantasy genre, make use of sculpted type. Note how these do not lack for personality, and yet, are more legible overall than the identities for bands.

3. Ginger Monkey, 4. Andreas Grey, 7. Jason Thornton. 1, 2, 5, 6, 8-11 unknown.

Sculpted type is a favorite of the beverage industry, for both alcoholic and non-alcoholic products.

Sculpted type is also popular in restaurant identities. Here, the association is with old-fashioned values, although sculpted type can also look contemporary. Either formality or informality can be communicated with this treatment. Sculpted type can be typographic fun.

Restaurants are places of relaxation and good times. Sculpted type can add to that feeling and can look either old-fashioned or contemporary. Credits: 4 Scott Greci; 10 Alan Ariail. All others unknown.

Credits: 1-2 Alan Ariail. All others unknown.

Credits: 1 - 3 Alan Ariail. All others unknown.

The food industry is a heavy user of this technique. Many artists don't even start with existing fonts and most do not use Type Warp tools. Instead, product wordmarks are often hand-drawn, and highly customized, even though ultimately rendered in vector.

Sculpted type has probably entered the subconscious of all of us. Many of us begin our days looking at sculpted type on the breakfast table without even thinking about it.

Sculpted Type is here to stay. It's not what's needed for all wordmarks, but when it works well, it is a remarkable technique.

Honing One's Craft

The preceding ten Visual Tehniques are just ways of isolating an approach to identity design. They are not etched in stone but are merely ways of seeing new possibilities.

I find it helpful to review them often, especially when I do not feel inspired in my particular approach for a given new identity project. Naturally, they will get easier with practice, most of them are within reach of almost any designer and, if done well, will be an improvement over the design at hand.

One of the joys of any creative field is to see one's own ablilities grow and to have new horizons give us greater vision.

Core Principles

Color, Typographic and Spatial Issues

Even superior designs can be undermined
by poor color, typographic or spatial choices.
How to prevent that.

Chapter 40

Logo and Signature Color Basics

Every identity must first work in solid black and white (1). There are too many situations to ignore where this constraint is a reality. Newspapers and the Yellow Pages don't do well with halftones, especially when the size is small. Businesses often print forms in black only, and some businesses have many forms. A solid black-and-white original will always reproduce better in photocopies and faxes than a color one.

Besides, as was mentioned in previous chapters, when color is allowed to dictate designs, it can be a distraction that allows esthetically inferior forms, proportions and shape refinements to slip by unnoticed, at least initially. Sooner or later, however, shoddy work will be recognized for what it is.

Unless an identity is a wordmark, it will be made up of a monogram or logo and a signature. Both elements together, not the logo alone, make up the identity.

Signatures should always get the greater contrast (2). This may seem counter-intuitive, because the logo typically takes much more time to design than the signature, but this rule remains valid. Why? Because the signature *must* be read. A logo is useful only if a viewer has seen it before and has learned to associate it with a company. On the other hand, if the signature can be read, it has communicated, even for a first-time viewer. This is true with both positive and reversed versions of an identity (3); the signature still receives the greater contrast.

The vast majority of identities use a black signature to assure readability; and black gives the maximum contrast on white backgrounds. This might inspire the unwise to seek some other color for the signature "just to be different." But any reason to use some other color than black must be really crucial to not be a bad bargain in the long run.

Even if an identity has a color logo and a color signature, the signature should have no less than a 60% contrast with any background (4). A logo may have less contrast than a signature, but never less than 40%. This provides a natural hierarchy in the identity in terms of contrast: first the signature and second the logo.

Color can be an important part of an identity, and every logo should be able to work in some color (5). When applying color, the signature still gets the greater contrast, whether the identity is used positive or reversed (6).

But remember this inescapable fact: a color is also a value. A medium-red could be equivalent to a 50% gray, and might be used equally well for the logo in a positive or reversed identity (5, 6).

Since a signature needs at least 60% contrast, it is absolutely impossible to achieve that on a 50% value background. Also, a mid-value background will almost always kill the contrast with a logo (7). Therefore, mid-value backgrounds should be avoided wherever possible. When this is not possible, the only viable solution is to use an all-white identity (8).

If the color of a logo is darker than 60% in a positive identity (9), it will not work in reverse (10).

One alternative is to use an all-white identity reversed out of the corporate color (11).

But for true reversal versions, many companies employ an alternative corporate color. It should not be just a tint of the original color (12) as the color will feel washed out. This is because white is totally neutral, and making a tint of any color naturally de-saturates it. A less saturated color will have a different emotional impact compared to the original color.

An alternative reverse color version should keep the same degree of saturation, even if the hue is adjusted a bit to achieve an appropriately lighter value (13).

Chapter 41

Advanced Color Issues for Identities

Color Contrast

An identity needs to work in all situations, not just in ideal lighting or at optimal distances. It must be easily recognizable in compromised lighting or less-than-ideal reproduction. What might look great on your computer monitor can (and most likely will) look different when printed. This is especially true with blues; they invariably print much darker than they appear on screen. Unless you print on the same machine every time, there will always be variances. Even printers of the same brand will vary in color output (see page 24).

This is why you can't cheat on or be careless about contrast as it appears on your monitor. The bare minimum contrast must be 40%. Why put your client's identity in jeopardy of being hard to read?

Some think they are safe from color variations when designing for the web, but they are not. It used to be that you could design web materials favoring the PC monitor gamma, secure in the knowledge that most viewers would see things as they were intended.

Not any longer. Every year Apple sales (including iPhones and iPads) have increased to the point that a designer who favors only the PC monitor gamma setting will miss about half the market. Contrasts that look okay on one screen may not work on another.

For all these reasons, which should not surprise any professional designer, corporate identity design needs to include "contrast insurance." You absolutely cannot say that "close enough" will work, given all the many variables surrounding where an identity will be used.

The contrast for a particular blue may look "good enough" on the screen, but blues almost always print darker than they show on screen. This is how this identity appeared in a glossy magazine print ad. Should a client be satisfied with an identity that doesn't show up?

As was mentioned in the previous chapter, a logo can have as little as a 40% difference with its background. But a color with only 40% contrast on white will have less contrast on a background such as pink or light blue – perhaps only 10% or 20%. Colors lighter than 40% will not provide enough contrast on white backgrounds and will be nearly invisible on any other light backgrounds.

Colors darker than 80% are easily mistaken for black because of printing variances, so the client pays for color but does not get the benefit.

Reversals on black should also follow the same 40% guideline. Very few colors will work reasonably well for both positive and reverse situations. Even so, if the background isn't black, but a dark color, the 40% difference should still be maintained.

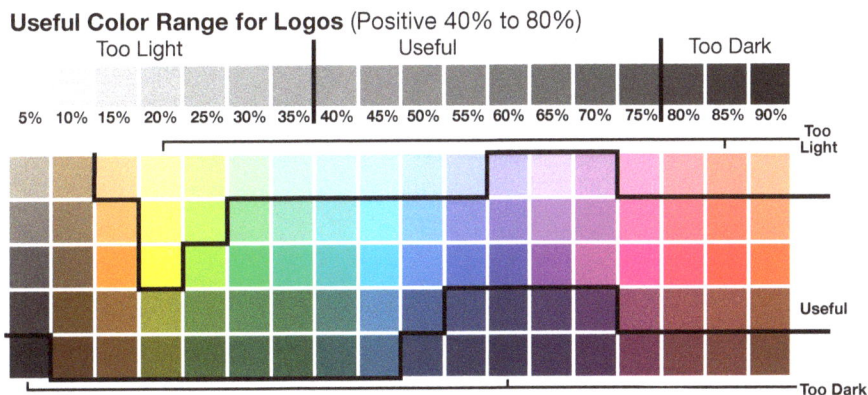

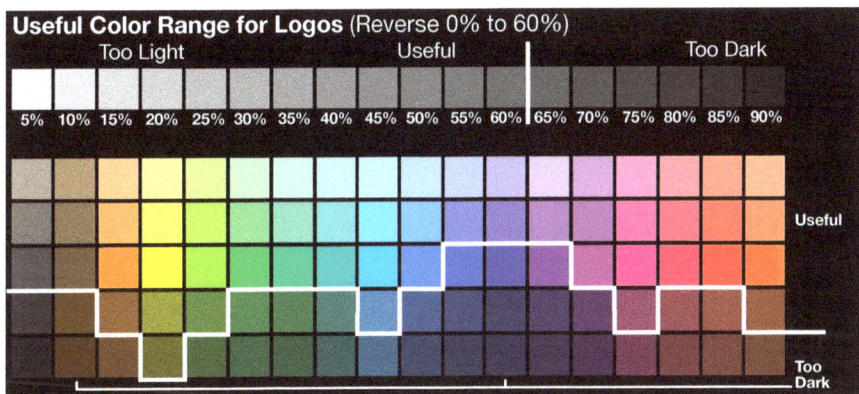

Useful Color Range for Logos (Positive 40% to 80%)

Too Light   Useful   Too Dark

| 5% | 10% | 15% | 20% | 25% | 30% | 35% | 40% | 45% | 50% | 55% | 60% | 65% | 70% | 75% | 80% | 85% | 90% |

Too Light

Useful

Too Dark

Useful Color Range for Logos (Reverse 0% to 60%)

Too Light   Useful   Too Dark

| 5% | 10% | 15% | 20% | 25% | 30% | 35% | 40% | 45% | 50% | 55% | 60% | 65% | 70% | 75% | 80% | 85% | 90% |

Useful

Too Dark

As has already been mentioned, the most common practice in identity design is to use color for the logo and black for the signature. If the signature gets a color other than black, it is important to remember these two principles:

1. The signature gets the greater contrast.

2. There should be a noticeable difference in value between the logo and signature colors.

If a value difference of about 20% is used, the widest range of color combinations is possible. In these cases, the lighter color needs to be in the range of 40% to 50%, and the darker color in the range of 60% to 100% (as in a black signature). When a non-corporate color is used as a background, the wisest practice is to reverse an identity in white against any color dark-enough to provide appropriate contrast.

No color identity will work on every value of background. Logo colors at about 50% value may work equally well in positive and reverse, but only if the backgrounds are white or 10% or, alternatively, black or 90% respectively. As a result, many companies will have one corporate color that is used for white and light backgrounds, and a similar but lighter alternative for reversals on dark backgrounds.

Designers who use an inappropriate color, like a bright, process yellow, because of some association with the product will find that it just doesn't work on white backgrounds. This is one reason that using the three "primary colors" never works in identities.

The whole identity in black only

The whole identity in the corporate color; must be at least a 60% value to give signature contrast.

Color logo and black signature

Two color identity, must be noticeable value difference; logo 40%-50%, signature 60%-80%

Reversed out of the corporate color; best if it is at least 60% value

Lighter color reversed out of the darker color, signature in white

Black and white reversed

Lighter color logo reversed out of black with white signature

Whole identity in lighter color reversed out of black

Whole identity in white on any dark enough non-corporate color

In the chart shown here, the corporate color is used for the logo alone and black for the signature (top of 1st column). The result will be a range of compatible backgrounds that will give the 40% contrast needed.

If the corporate color is at least a 60% value, it may be used for both logo and signature (top, 2nd and 3rd columns), but even with an 80% value, only a narrow range of backgrounds will give the minimum 60% contrast needed for the signature.

Generally speaking, mid-value backgrounds should be avoided. It can be impossible to obtain enough contrast between such a background and any corporate color. When mid-value backgrounds cannot be avoided, often only an all-white version of the identity will give enough contrast (4th column). Remember that the cutoff for reversal vs. surprint is not at 50% background value, but at 35%.

Questor Marine	Questor Marine	Questor Marine	Questor Marine	0%
Questor Marine	Questor Marine	Questor Marine	Questor Marine	10%
Questor Marine	No Appropriate Variation	No Appropriate Variation	Questor Marine	20%
Questor Marine	No Appropriate Variation	No Appropriate Variation	Questor Marine	30%
No Appropriate Variation	No Appropriate Variation	No Appropriate Variation	Questor Marine	40%
No Appropriate Variation	No Appropriate Variation	No Appropriate Variation	Questor Marine	50%
No Appropriate Variation	No Appropriate Variation	No Appropriate Variation	Questor Marine	60%
No Appropriate Variation	No Appropriate Variation	No Appropriate Variation	Questor Marine	70%
Questor Marine	No Appropriate Variation	No Appropriate Variation	Questor Marine	80%
Questor Marine	No Appropriate Variation	No Appropriate Variation	Questor Marine	90%
Questor Marine	Questor Marine	Questor Marine	Questor Marine	100%

Questor Aqua
Pantone 322
CMYK:
C90, M45, Y30, K0
RGB:
R66, G120, B151
Hexidecimal:
427897
Vinyl:
Avery Nautical Blue
A8650-O

Questor Reverse Aqua
Pantone 121-7
CMYK:
C80, M0, Y20, K0
RGB:
R84 G182 B204
Hexidecimal:
5CABCA
Avery Peacock Blue

Many identities that use a darker color will require another corporate color for reversals. In the bottom of the first three columns, the "Alternate Questor Aqua" is used, but with the same contrast constraints: 40% for the logo, 60% for the signature.

AVERY Signage Films

A5 New Translucent Colors
(For Backlit Signs)

| Red A9340-T | Poinsettia A9343-T | Holly Green A9602-T | Cobalt Blue A9588-T |

A5 Translucent (For Backlit Signs)   **A8 Opaque** (For Opaque Signs and Vehicles)   **A9 Opaque PANTONE® Colors** (For Opaque Signs and Vehicles)   **A9 Translucent PANTONE® Colors** (For Backlit Signs)

A5 Translucent	A8 Opaque			A8 Opaque cont.		A9 Opaque PANTONE®		A9 Translucent PANTONE®	
White A5001-T	White A8001-O	Imitation Gold A8250-O	Warm Red A8305-O	Periwinkle A8510-O	Aquamarine A8633-O	Warm Gray 1 C A9021-O / Yellow 012 C A9111-O / Process Cyan C A9583-O	White (not) A9189-T / Orange 021 C A9189-T / 3005 C A9561-T
Black A5090-T	Matte White A8002-O	Parchment A8205-O	Tomato Red A8325-O	Copenhagen A8505-O	Real Teal A8615-O	Warm Gray 2 C A9113-O / 109 C A9113-O / 299 C A9577-O	Cool Gray 2 C A9082-T / 1655 C A9161-T / 285 C A9526-T
Brown A5295-T	Clear A8003-O	Almond A8210-O	Fire Red A8345-O	Dark Navy Blue A8597-O	Dark Aqua A8605-O	Cool Gray 1 C A9081-O / 123 C A9117-O / 285 C A9526-O	Cool Gray 1 C A9011-T / 472 C A9318-T / 279 C A9505-T
Rust Brown A5280-T	Matte Clear A8004-O	Beige A8220-O	Cardinal red A8330-O	Dark Blue A8595-O	Seafoam A8603-O	Cool Gray 2 C A9082-O / 116 C A9114-O / 279 C A9503-O	Cool Gray 3 C A9069-T / 877 C A9302-T / 290 C A9566-T
Chartreuse A5103	Light Gray A8010-O	Dark Beige A8230-O	Dark Red A8350-O	Light Navy A8590-O	Spectra Everglade A8610-O	Cool Gray 3 C A9083-O / Orange 021 C A9189-O / 292 C A9557-O	430 C A9047-T / 1788 C A9302-T / Red 032 C A9306-T
Primrose Yellow A5110-T	Palm Oyster A8220-O	Sandstone A8265-O	Apple Red A8385-O	Shadow Blue A8520-O	Spruce Green A8640-O	Cool Gray 4 C A9064-O / Warm Red C A9323-O	Process Black C A9081-T / 186 C A9308-T / 321 C A9619-T
Pumpkin Orange A5183-T	Light Ash A8025-O	Buckskin A8270-O	Spectra Red A8360-O	Majestic Blue A8525-O	Teal A8620-O	Cool Gray 5 C A9085-O / 485 C A9321-O	277 C A9502-O / 200 C A9298-T / 322 C A9622-T
Cardinal Red A5530-T	Slate Gray A8030-O	Camel A8240-O	Burgundy A8370-O	Interstate Blue A8575-O	Dark Teal A8630-O	420 C A9008-O / Red 032 C A9306-O	290 C A9558-O / 4495 C A9275-T / 187 C A9355-T / 333 C A9616-T
Red A5340-T	Medium Gray A8035-O	Putty A8235-O	Burgundy Maroon A8370-O	Sapphire Blue A8580-O	Nautical Blue A8650-O	427 C A9011-O / 185 C A9307-O	304 C A9581-O / 188 C A9249-T / 188 C A9368-T / Green C A9642-T
Vivid Rose A5414-T	Pewter A8050-O	Butter A8105-O	Coral A8405-O	Vivid Blue A8570-O	Dark Ivy A8650-O	429 C A9012-O / Rubine Red C A9347-O	333 C A9616-O / A9252-T / A-9T / A9634-T
Pink Lavender A5407-T	Dark Gray A8055-O	Canary Yellow A8120-O	Light Magenta A8410-O	Intense Blue A8585-O	Vibrant Green A8655-O	877 C A9089-O / Process Magenta C A9411-O	Green C A9642-O / 155251 C A8-T / 214 C A9252-T / 354 C A9626-T
Light Baby Blue A5537-T	Medium Marine Gray A8060-O	Medium Yellow A8130-O	Blossom A8415-O	Medium Blue A8555-O	Apple Green A8660-O	Process Black C A9081-O / Violet C A9413-O	480 C A9403-T / 2622 C A9448-T / 355 C A9662-T
Bright Blue A5567-T	Battleship Gray A8070-O	Sunflower A8140-O	Magenta A8430-O	Olympic Blue A8530-O	Kelly Green A8670-O	466 C A9252-O / Reflex Blue C A9579-O	375 C A9634-O / 7500 C A9217-T / 266 C A9460-T / 349 C A9663-T
Twilight Blue A5591-T	Matte Black A8080-O	Dark Yellow A8150-O	Raspberry A8435-O	Light Blue A8540-O	Bright Green A8685-O	488 C A9255-O / Blue 072 C A9501-O	347 C A9617-O / 100 C A9113-T / 274 C A9467-T / 7483 C A9678-T
Ocean Blue A5535-T	Black A8090-O	Apricot A8155-O	Plum A8440-O	Peacock Blue A8545-O	Forest Green A8685-O	155 C A9251-O / 286 C A9528-O	109 C A9113-T / 261 C A9588-T
Tidewater A5007-T	Brown A8295-O	Orange A8160-O	Deep Purple A8450-O	Powder Blue A8550-O	Deep Green A8690-O	100 C A9112-O / 293 C A9559-O	Yellow 012 C A9111-T / 2747 C A9593-T
Shamrock A5671-T	Cocoa A8278-O	Bright Orange A8180-O	Purple A8465-O	Butterfly A8552-O	Dark Green A8690-O	Process Yellow C A9106-O / 300 C A9578-O	116 C A9114-T / 288 C A9584-T
Medium Green A5681-T	Terra Cotta A8260-O	Tangerine A8315-O	Lavender A8475-O	Cadet Blue A8515-O	Polo Green A895-O	Yellow C A9107-O / Process Blue C A9582-O	1235 C A9143-T / 2945 C A9566-T

Signage and Vehicles

Most businesses need signage or vehicles identified. Since signage and vehicle graphics are typically done in vinyl, it is a wise precaution to pick an identity color from one that is already available in vinyl. Not every color in the Pantone book comes in a matching vinyl, but you can get a matching Pantone ink for every standard vinyl color that exists. It makes sense, therefore, to work from vinyl colors before committing to any corporate identity color.

Custom vinyl colors can be made, but the client has to order thousands of rolls of such a color. While this may be fine for a national company, it is out of the question for a medium or small firm. Yes, one can get full-color printed vinyl, but again, even though the initial cost is the same as standard-cut vinyl, process-printed vinyl isn't as colorfast and, as of this writing, only lasts about a third as long as cut vinyl. For companies with large fleets of vehicles, this is no small financial consideration.

After choosing a vinyl color, it is a simple matter to identify the equivalents in Pantone inks, CMYK, RGB and Hexidecimal. This will enable a corporate identity to be as consistent as possible across different media.

Remember, a professional works in the client's best interests, and any decision that will incur added expense should be the client's decision, not the designer's.

CLARK
CONSULTING SERVICES

This logo was featured in a design annual as an innovative design. It isn't. Not only does it not reproduce in black only, it also has internal contrast problems. And besides all that, it needs black plus three shades of olive green, two of which are not available in solid vinyl.

Internal Contrast

Another factor that too many designers fail to consider is internal contrast. Here again, a 40% minimum contrast is needed between touching elements. If you use black for containing shapes, for instance, colors used for fill need to be 60% or lighter to provide the minimum internal contrast of 40%.

The identity above is legible in black. In the color-filled version, two of the fill colors are too dark to give sufficient internal contrast. The red is marginal at best, and the blue is way too dark to be easily distinguished from the black. This can be corrected by substituting colors lighter than a 60% value, which will gives the 40% minimum difference needed with the black containing shapes.

Busy Backgrounds

Boston Pizza redid its identity a few years ago. It was not an improvement. It would have been far better for the circle containing the monogram BP to have been plain white. The new logo has a built-in busy background, which makes it very hard to read at a distance, whereas properly designed logos are quite readable at a dictance.

Beyond that, the brown building background is close in value to the red signature, making it vanish. Altogether, very difficult to see and a massive expenditure for that company to end up with a worse identity than its former identity.

Difficulties with Reversals

Most logos can be used in reverse without any problem. However, if the logo imagery makes use of values to indicate three-dimensional solid with highlights and shadows, a reversal will not give the desired effect. Another difficulty occurs when part of the logo represents something that must be light; switching that element to dark in the reversed version will, again, not give the desired effect.

The former AT&T logo could not be used as a straight reversal because it would look like the Death Star from Star Wars. Instead, a unique variation was designed for use in reversal situations that avoided this appearance. The KFC logo if reversed looked like an X-ray; they had to use a positive face over the reversal background. The lighthouse below looks like it broadcasts darkness in a true reversal. Here also, an alternate positive logo was inserted into the reversal background.

Original Positive
Logos

Accurate but
Inappropriate Reversals

Adjusted Reversal
Versions

Chapter 42

Typographic Issues with Brand Signatures

nutella
Miele
TOSHIBA
Canon®
TAMPAX®

Neutrogena®
PENTAX
cacharel
maxell®
COVERGIRL®
marie claire

Pentel®
Nikon®
ILFORD
NOKIA
DIESEL

For our purposes, we've defined a signature as the company name written in a particular font, with minimal or no design adjustments. As was stated before, this is the least value-added design and has been used historically mostly for identities of consumer products. Signatures are not as suitable for other kinds of corporate identities.

For most companies the normal practice is to either have a wordmark, with some unique design element, or to have a signature accompany a logo or a monogram. In that case, the signature follows our original definition: the company's functional name written in a particular font.

Westinghouse   AT&T   HONDA   Wilson

UNITED   NBC   Columbia

CHANEL   MINOLTA   adidas   COREL

crocs™   TARGET   SHOWTIME®

BRAUN   CONAIR   zippo

119

Trendy vs. Timeless

Many designers will want to use a distinctive or trendy font in a signature. It's natural that we don't want our signature to look like so many others. But that's not what we see in the best identities. Why? Because you don't want your signature type to look passé in a few years. So if you use the latest "in" font, chances are it will look tired before long. Many companies have learned this the hard way. We should learn it the easy way, by benefiting from their experience.

Remember, the more personality a font has, the more likely it is to become dated and look tired. Many companies that used the more idiosyncratic fonts have had to redesign their identities to look contemporary. Unfortunately, looking contemporary is what led them to that problem in the first place. What is needed instead is a look that is timeless.

Ask yourself, "Will this font stand the test of time?" That is what a good signature should do.

Each of these signatures has been redesigned to use type that will look less dated in a few years. Not all of them have succeeded.

Legibility Above All

Some designers think it's leading edge to be ultra-modern or even cryptic with their signature designs. But it is just bleeding edge, not leading edge—rather like gluing thumbtacks point-up on a saddle, thinking they will keep the rider from falling off. For the public, the effort to decipher these signatures becomes painful and may not be worth the bother.

The absolute first requirement of a signature font is clarity. One might conceive of a seesaw with clarity on one end and personality on the other. If personality goes up, clarity most often goes down. Scripts, for instance, are among the most difficult font groups to read instantly. There is a reason we see so few "fancy" fonts used in identity design. Typically, the fancier the font, the lower the readability.

Another reason to opt for type with less personality is that you don't want the signature vying with the logo or monogram for attention. The logo should attract and engage the eye, while the signature identifies whose logo it is. If the signature has too much personality, there will be a tug-of-war for the viewer's attention.

What were these designers thinking? Did they imagine that people wanted to play a guessing game? The last two samples on the right are not totally illegible, but neither has their treatment promoted instant readability, which should be the goal in all branding design.

Signature Weight

Since clarity is essential if an identity is to do its most basic job, there are real drawbacks to a signature with no mass (see Deadly Sin of Logo Design #2: Lack of Mass). When signatures with no mass are used in a small space, the signature's legibility will be compromised. Even worse, when–not if–an identity is used in reverse, the signature's letterforms will fill in, no matter what kind of printing is used. While signage in cut vinyl will not fill in when reversed, it is usually viewed at a distance, which will have the same visual effect.

This issue does not go away on the Web. Because there are only 72 pixels per inch (nominally) on the Web, very fine strokes don't show up as solid black (or white when reversed). This can mean that none of the pixels of a uniform-stroke typeface (as in Dax Light) or a thick-and-thin-stroke typeface (as in Bodoni) will show up as black or white respectively.

Signature
Signature
Signature
Signature
Signature
Signature
Signature

Signature **Signature**
Signature Signature
Signature Signature
Signature Signature

Signature **Signature**
Signature Signature
Signature Signature
Signature Signature

Signatures are easier to read at a distance or at small sizes if the type has some mass. Fonts with both thick and very thin strokes also suffer especially when printed in reverse. This problem does not go away on the web, where thin strokes are so small that the pixels making them are neither the pure foreground nor the pure background color.

Kerning

Even though a signature with a logo or monogram is just type set in a particular font, you can't use it without perfect kerning. Kerning means adjusting the spaces between letters so that they appear uniform. While this is not done for body copy text, it becomes extremely important in identity signatures. These words will be seen at all different sizes and over a long period of time, and clumsy spacing can become quite noticeable, even irksome, if proper kerning is not done.

One simple way to discover where kerning is most needed is to look at words upside-down. Even better, look at them upside-down and backwards, perhaps through a piece of paper. Instead of noticing the letters, you then should notice any uneven spaces between them. To achieve good kerning, it is often acceptable to let two letters touch or even overlap. Indeed, many signatures have tight letter spacing to begin with, so that all or most of the letters touch anyway.

If you are inexperienced at kerning, you can try printing your proposed signature in larger and very small sizes. Notice whether there are any kerning issues.

Much will depend on the particular letter combinations. Capital Ws and Ts, for instance, may need other letters nestling under their overhanging parts. Capital Ls naturally make a large void on the right and are prime candidates for joined ligatures with the next letter (see Visual Technique #6: Ligatures, Swashes and Flourishes). The possible combinations and needs for kerning are as varied as the words in our language.

Proper Type Kerning
Proper Type Kerning
Proper Type Kerning

The key to proper kerning is to equalize the negative spaces between letters. Viewing a line of type upside down makes it easier to see problem areas. Identity typography must have excellent kerning.

Examples of poor kerning are all about us. Look at those gaps! But sometimes over-kerning can be a problem, too, as seen in the two disastrous samples in the lower right. The better solution to a capital "L" followed by capital "I" can be easily solved by using lower case letters instead of all caps.

Signatures and Extra Letter-spacing

It has become trendy to add extra letter-spacing to signatures (called tracking in most graphics software). Generally speaking, this is a counter-productive design decision, for two reasons:

1. Extra letter-spacing makes a word read less naturally, visually speaking. The words don't hold together as well.

2. Extra letter-spacing makes the signature type smaller in the same horizontal space than it would have been with normal or even tight tracking.

Graphic design always has space limitations: page size, ad widths, column widths, and so on. To ignore this fact of our profession is absurd. It is equally unrealistic to think that size doesn't matter, at least as far as legibility is concerned. If signature type is smaller than it needs to be, it will, therefore, become illegible sooner than a signature with normal tracking.

The length of a signature has a direct bearing on the danger of extra letter-spacing. As you can see, more tracking merely weakens a medium-size signature but can be disastrous for long signatures. In the end, only short signatures survive this treatment, (there are many successful ones in use now), but that doesn't mean it improves readability.

Letterspacing

L e t t e r s p a c i n g

L e t t e r s p a c i n g

Letterspacing

L e t t e r s p a c i n g

L e t t e r s p a c i n g

Letterspacing

L e t t e r s p a c i n g

L e t t e r s p a c i n g

Letterspacing

L e t t e r s p a c i n g

Letterspacing

Here we have a word set with natural letterspacing, then with typical extra letterspacing, which widens out the horizontal space it requires. Third we have reduced the word with the extra letterspacing to fit in the same horizontal width as the original word. Type with extra tracking or extra letterspacing will be much smaller vertically in the same horizontal space, and therefore be harder to read than when using natural letterspacing.

Short

M e d i u m

L e n g t h e n e d

Short

M e d i u m

L e n g t h e n e d

S h o r t

M e d i u m

L e n g t h e n e d

Extra tracking is more harmful to longer signatures than to shorter ones.

Extended, Regular or Condensed Type?

A separate but related issue is type width. Any font will have an overall aspect. Either it is inherently condensed, regular or extended.

Very long signatures will work better if set in more condensed fonts. If set in regular width fonts they will be vertically shorter for their width. If set in extended fonts they tend to be very short vertically for their width. As we have already established, when a signature is wider than it needs to be horizontally, it will also be shorter vertically, and accordingly, harder to read. Therefore, long signatures benefit most from condensed fonts and benefit least from extended fonts.

On the other hand, shorter signatures have the flexibility to use fonts of any aspect. Medium-length signatures are less flexible, but could be successful with all three width aspects of fonts.

Interminable
Helvetica Neue LT Std Medium Condensed

Interminable
Helvetica Neue LT Std Medium

Interminable
Helvetica Neue LT Std Medium Extended

Interminable Interminable
Interminable Interminable
Interminable Interminable

Here is the same word set in the same weight but in different widths. The extended version is much shorter for the width than the regular or condensed versions. Therefore, condensed fonts should be considered for long signatures while extended fonts should be avoided.

Short Short Short
Short Short Short
Short Short Short

**UPPER CASE WORDS VARY LESS
lower case words vary more**

All Caps vs. Upper and Lower Case

Many studies have been done on the relative legibility of all capital letters versus upper and lower case. These studies measured instant recognition of words on highway billboards, where a viewer might be able to spare a mere second or less to look while driving. The studies showed that words in upper and lower case were easier to read than those in all caps.

Does this have implications for identity design?

Given that instant recognition is a fundamental goal of any identity design, it should. Consider also that some difficult kerning issues (L followed by A,

W followed by Y, etc.) are lessened or not an issue at all in lower case.

Does this mean that all caps are unsuitable for signature design? No. Many fine and successful signatures are in all caps. But it does mean that if a given word poses difficulties, a designer should always consider upper and lower case.

What about using all lower case?

In our Western culture we capitalize first letters of proper names, and a signature is definitely the proper name of a company, so the first inclination should be to use upper case for the first letter. Too often, new designers choose all lower case "just to be different." As we have discussed earlier, that is an immature reason if it doesn't make the design stronger.

Besides that, using all lower-case letters can make a name seem less worthy of respect. That is not to say that all lower-case signatures should never be done, but they should be done for esthetic reasons, not in an attempt to be trendy or avant garde.

at&t ▸ AT&T

nordnet ▸ Nordnet

CITIBANK ▸ citibank

personal group ▸ pg Personal Group

Lower case letters look less formal and also less important. It would be going too far to say they should never be used, but I would say there ought to be a concrete reason for using them, not just to be different or to be trendy.

Chapter 43

Spatial Issues with Identities

Visual Logic

Much of the good in a design, even in an exquisite design, can be undermined by poor spacing. There is no benefit to having size relationships that are jarring or spaces between elements that do not look natural.

Visual logic is one way to accomplish good spacing. That is simply that shapes and sizes that are repeated make visual sense to our eyes. They seem natural, expected, right.

Gaps or spaces between elements of an identity that are based on visual logic

don't call attention to themselves. After all, if the spaces drew one's attention instead of the elements, that would be counter-productive design as well.

One of the worst options is to have a space be indefinite. How can anyone know if they have the right spacing when the spaces have not been specified?

This is why it is important to make measurements not in millimeters or points or inches, but in units that come from the type itself. That way they are always repeatable, scalable and avoid complex math.

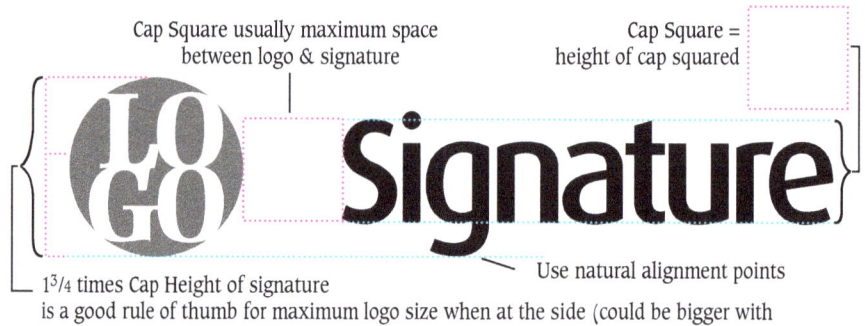

Cap Square usually maximum space between logo & signature

Cap Square = height of cap squared

1³/₄ times Cap Height of signature is a good rule of thumb for maximum logo size when at the side (could be bigger with

Use natural alignment points

Thickness of signature stroke is the minimum space between logo and signature

1¹/₄ times Cap Height of signature is a good rule of thumb for minimum logo size when at the side

Logo vs. Signature Sizes

Logos and Monograms usually require an accompanying signature. A logo and signature together constitute the identity. (A notable exception is Apple. When your company is as well-known as Apple, can you omit the signature.) Logos and signatures shouldn't fight each other. The beginning designer will naturally care more about the logo than the signature because that was the part that usually was more labor intensive compared with the signature. Some want to display the logo big and the signature small, but this is a mistake. There should be a harmony between logo and signature. Size relationships should be balanced.

When a logo is at the side of the signature it will generally look balanced if it is between 1¼ to 1¾ times the signature cap height. If it is smaller than that, it will appear insignificant. If the logo is much bigger than 1¾ times the signature height, it will appear to be eating the signature like PacMan gobbling its food. If the signature is longer, a larger logo may be justified.

Another factor is the amount of space between the logo and the signature. If the logo is too close, it will interfere with the instant reading of the signature, weakening the identity's effectiveness. If it is too far away, they will not feel connected. Another good rule of thumb for this space is between one cap height of the signature for a maximum distance and one or two time the thickness of the signature stroke for the minimum distance between the logo and signature.

When Logo is above:
Logo up to 2 times
Cap Height of
signature
(sometimes more
with a larger signature)

Maximum vertical space
is x-height of signature
May measure from
cap height or x-height

Cap
Height

Signature

x-height

Minimum size
1½ times
cap height
of signature

Minimum space
thickness of signature
Measured from
cap height

Cap
Height

Signature

x-height

When the logo is above the signature in a vertical format, the identity will usually look balanced when the logo is 1½ to 2 times the cap height of the signature.

A common vertical space between the logo and the signature is the x-height of the signature, starting from either the signature x-height or the cap height. The minimum space between the logo and signature is one or two times the thickness of the signature stroke measured from the cap height.

Other factors can influence what will look balanced including the size and weight of the signature. The number of words in the signature may also make a big difference. A two-word signature would need a larger logo when the signature words are stacked flush left with the logo at the side. If the signature is all caps it may need a proportionately larger logo to balance. Still, the above rules of thumb are good starting places.

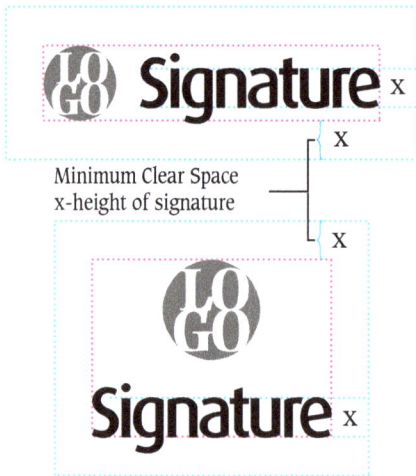

Minimum Clear Space
x-height of signature

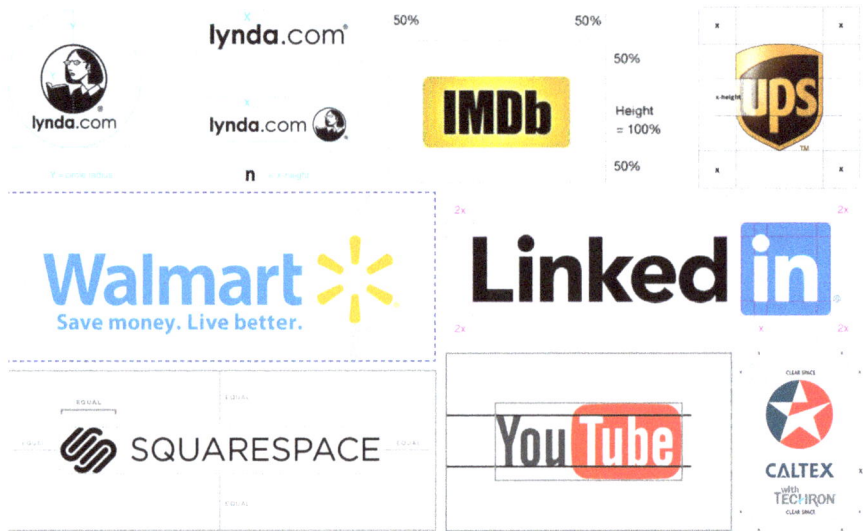

Clear Space

Every identity needs a certain amount of space that belongs to it alone. Nothing else may come into this Clear Space, not even the company's own return address on stationery, for instance. Clear space is measured from the outside of the perimeter of any parts of an identity. Individual signature descenders are sometimes excluded from this perimeter calculation or they may be included, as in the samples shown here. The Clear Space should never be less than the x-height of the signature. Many times, it is the cap height of the signature, occasionally, even more.

Notice that measurements for clear space—as well as all other spatial measurements—have been made *not* using inches, points, or millimeters. All measurements have been internal to the identity, such as the signature's x-height or cap height or stroke thickness. Not only does this make all measurements automatically scalable, but it also is a natural way to achieve visual logic.

It is a standard practice to have a clear space for all identities. Note that this is measured from the outer edge of the whole identity, not just the logo. Some companies shown here did not give their identities enough clear space. This will result in crowding the identity in various design situations, a visual disrespect to the identity. Recommended absolute minimum clear space is the signature's x-height.

128

Slogan vs. Corporate Activity Phrase

Many well-known companies have slogans that they incorporate into alternate variations of their corporate identity. These slogans tend to change over time according to new marketing directions. Some examples are:

McDonald's	I'm lovin' it
FedEx	When there is no tomorrow
IBM	Solutions for a smart planet
Coca-Cola	Open Happiness
Nike	Just do it
KFC	Finger Lickin' Good

But slogans are not for everyone; they only work for companies that are so well-known that they don't need to tell people what they do or companies whose name is so descriptive that there is no need to explain further.

All other companies should *not* use a slogan; what they need instead is a Corporate Activity Phrase (CA Phrase for short), some brief word or words that explain what they do.

When I was a teen I saw trucks driving around with the name "Purolator" on them and nothing else. What's a Purolator? I thought maybe they made machines that made really good tasting coffee by filtering it (percolator / pure-olator?). Apparently I wasn't the only one who didn't know who they were or what they did because a few years later, they began to include the single word "courier" on their truck identities. That's a corporate activity phrase (or CA Phrase). It is important in out-of-context situations, like on vehicles and signage.

A business named Murphy's could be a men's clothier, a restaurant or a funeral home. Without a corporate activity phrase included with their identity, much of their advertising, especially that on vehicles or signage is largely wasted. If I don't already know what Murphy's does, and see their vehicle, I still won't know without a corporate activity phrase. The key is that they must be simple and clear. Examples might include:

Tax Consultants
Industrial Robotics
Pharmaceuticals
Natural Foods
Divorce Lawyers
Hydrogen Fueled Engines

For any businesses like these––and a million other ones not as famous as FedEx—a CA Phrase (not a slogan) should be incorporated into the identity for use whenever it is out of context or when a viewer might not already know what the company does. It goes on business cards, but perhaps not on the letterhead (because the letter can explain that better, if needed). It goes on signage and vehicle graphics. It goes on ads and brochures.

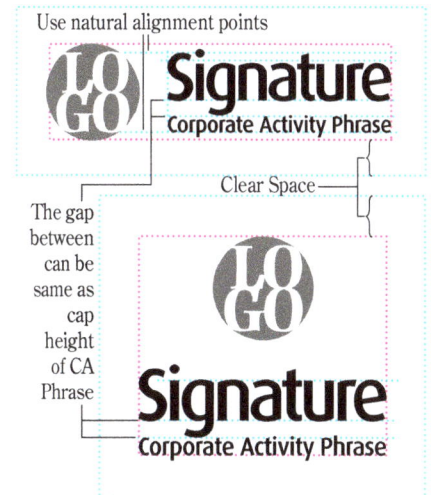

When a corporate activity phrase is used, it is considered part of the identity. The best place for it is under and smaller than the signature. It should be in the same color as the signature to avoid drawing undo attention to itself. The ideal spacing is to have a gap between it and the signature equal to the corporate activity phrase's own cap height. That spacing always works, depending on the existence and depth of any signature descenders and on the length and height of the activity phrase. It comes back to visual logic.

Logo Aspect

Wordmarks tend to be much wider than they are tall. And there are successful logos of just about any shape: tall, wide, irregular, etc. Even so, there is a natural advantage to having a logo with close to equal height and width. Squares and circles, for instance, are more versatile than shapes much more extreme in aspect. That doesn't mean they can't be used; it just means they are less versatile in different design layout situations.

When these principles of visual logic are practiced with care, there is usually an increased esthetic appeal added to any identity design.

One of the advantages of having a logo separate from a signature is that there can be different arrangements. Logos with the same vertical and horizontal dimensions (or close to it) are inherently easier to work along with a signature than a logo of extreme aspect.

Implementing Core Principles of Identity Design

Hundreds of current examples
demonstrate the consequences of deviating
from the Core Principles of Branding and the
benefits of redesigning an identity to be in conformity with them.

Chapter 44

The Danger of Following Trends Blindly

The Problem with Trends

Search online for the term "logo design trends" and you can see what designers all over the world are doing now for corporate identity design. But how can you really know if the things you see in these sources are good examples or bad? Do today's designers follow each other like so many lemmings, finding comfort in company, but having no real direction based on independent and time-proven principles?

Many of the poor examples I have shown in this book I saw first in respected design magazines displayed as supposed good design. Most of the books on corporate identity design show lots of logos, but does that mean that they are all good and worthy of emulation?

If you have teenagers learning to drive, would you tell them all they need to do is look at what other drivers do on the road? Or would you insist that they learn from a bona fide driving instructor or school—or at least get the official Department of Motor Vehicles regulations and study them?

Anyone can hang out their shingle declaring to the world that they are graphic designers or even branding designers. Do they even have any design training? And is all graphic design training equal? Does coming through a famous school guarantee anything?

I witnessed a huge change in graphic design education over the twenty-five years I taught graphic design in college. When I began as a designer and even when I began to teach, there were specific manual skills and design sensitivities that *had* to be mastered. Back then there were whole professions

that existed to support the graphic design industry. Typesetters, stat camera operators and photoengravers were jobs that are almost non-existent now.

Why?

Because of the personal computer. Now graphic designers are their own typesetters, do their own scans, and nobody even makes color separations any more for printing. It's just part of the digital output supplied by our computers.

Graphic design education has had to devote significant time to teaching students the software that they must learn to use. Photoshop, Illustrator and InDesign are the bare minimum and all are vast and intricate programs. Subjects like Color Theory, Art History, Design History and Illustration, that used to be an integral part of the standard graphic design curriculum, are today often considered expendable.

The result is that few design students are even considering principles now, let alone being schooled in them. We are in the second generation of digital design, so even the instructors of the current generation never got that exposure themselves.

Does that mean that there are no principles in design, specifically branding design?

No, of course not. There are indeed principles. That is what this book is all about.

But you won't learn those principles from following the trends. That is like the proverbial blind leading the blind.

"The Blind Leading the Blind" by Peter Bruegel the Elder, 1568

Does that mean thatwe should become design hermits and not look about at what is being done?

No.

But it would be advisable to always ask if the example in question will work in the myriad of media and situations that a corporate identity must work in, and if it will reproduce consistently.

As we have already demonstrated, a company may discover that their identity does not meet their needs. We will see that many companies and the designers they hire are feeling their way along. Indeed the whole design industry has been feeling its way along to make logos that last, that stand the test of time.

To a large extent, this has been by trial and error. And those errors can be so costly. But over time, they lead designers to avoid the very things that we mentioned in chapters 21 through 27, the Seven Deadly Sins of Logo Design.

We will see in the next seven chapters how many companies have redesigned their identities to be in conformity with the Core Principles of Branding Design and to avoid the Seven Deadly Sins of Logo Design.

Why?

Because ignoring them just doesn't work.

Chapter 45

Deadly Sin of Logo Design #1 Fixed:

Able to Work in Solid Black

(Or Any Contrasting Color)

Flat Color Wins

So many companies that had either multicolored logos or logos that required gradients or a halftone screen have realized that there are just too many situations where their identities did not reproduce properly or clearly or without extra expense. From vehicles (where printed vinyl doesn't last as long) to stationery (which is often printed on smaller presses) to the separate issue of basic clarity.

Many companies have changed their logos to work in one flat color (which means, of course, that they could work in solid black as well).

With many of these examples, issues other than color are also addressed to good effect.

It might seem counter-intuitive to the inexperienced, but a single flat color is inherently clearer than any multicolored variation.

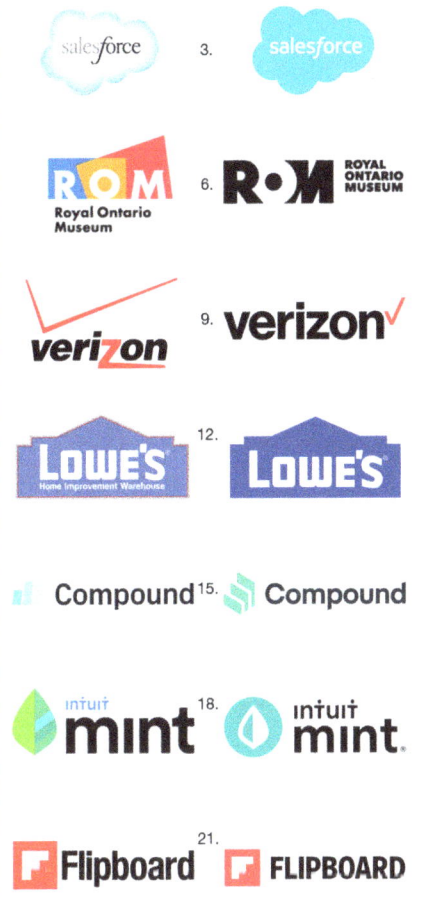

1. BT traded its multicolored logo for a rather boring identity instead, but at least this one will be clear and easy to reproduce consistently. 2. DC Comics' new logo is also simpler, and this one has more mass than BT's. 3. Salesforce's old logo subordinated the signature inside a soft cloud shape with half of their type being low contrast. In addition to stronger type, the logo will now be easier to reproduce. In the future, will they reduce the cloud shape to a separate logo and make their signature black? 4. The old logo looks like it was designed more by an engineer than a designer. The new one is solid, but the monogram could use some color. 5. By omitting the drop shadow type and the red field, Netflix gained a stronger and larger wordmark. 6. ROM's logo now can be used in any color with sufficient contrast. 7. Hootsuite gained clarity and impact by going with a flat color logo and they fixed their signature contrast issue. 8. Taco Bell's new logo has much better contrast and is easier to recognize. 9. Verizon removed its red "z" from the middle of their wordmark and went with a smaller checkmark logo at the end of their signature. 10. Southwest Airlines got rid of their airplane illustration–which should never have been used as a logo–with a tidy heart logo. They can improve it further by removing the light grey halo around the logo or better yet, just use the heart in one color. 11. MailChimp's single-color logo is much easier to see and recognize than its multicolor version. 12. Lowe's updated logo omitted the red border and darkened the blue to make it more effective. 13. Mack Truck's chrome hood ornament logo might have seemed cool but the new solid color logo is much clearer. 14. Axway may have been trying to look like Xerox's 2008 logo. It didn't work any better than Xerox's logo did. Axway's new logo and single color signature are more solid. 15. Even though Compound is an online business where some might suppose the rules about one color logos don't apply, they saw that their multi-colored logo looked weak and changed it for the better. 16. As with Compound, Formstack, another online business, sees that a single color logo is more effective. 17. Ford, like Mack, experimented with the chrome look and went back to their flat logo with a slightly dimensional variation when needed. 18. Intuit Mint is the third online business to conform to the principle that single color logos are stronger. 19. Even simple outlining, which might have been thought to improve contrast, is better removed. 20. Yet another online business finds greater clarity in a single color logo and a signature in a single weight. 21. Flipboard, an online news aggregator, gave up its logo with two pink tints. By simply making the logo flat red and white, it is greatly improved.

Chapter 46

Deadly Sin of Logo Design #2 Fixed:

Having Sufficient Mass

Delicate Doesn't Work

Corporate identity design is different from every other area of graphic design in that the end product must work in a wide variety of circumstances, be readable even at small sizes and be reproduced in every conceivable medium. For that reason, graphic approaches that might be appropriate in other design situations may not work in identity design. On this page the chapter title is in Helvetica Neue LT Std Thin. It is elegant and works well in this situation, but as thin as it is, it would be a poor choice for identity design.

A company's identity will be featured on signs, meaning they will be viewed at a distance. Visual elements that don't have a certain minimum of mass are just not as visible as those that do have mass. There's no getting away from it.

1. Phillips had their light-weight logo for forty years before fixing the mass issue. 2. When Macy's added the star logo to their identity, they also opted for delicate type. After fifteen years they fixed that with a heavier version of the same font. 3. Covergirl had a thin humanist font for eighteen years before finally giving their signature more mass. 4. Big Nerd Ranch fixed contrast issues and gave their logo and signature some mass. 5. Donkey Sanctuary replaced almost invisible thin lines with solid planar shapes. 6. Yahoo! made a major improvement with it's signature by adding mass.

7. Skyscanner has a much more visible identity with an improved logo and signature. 8. Huffington Post made two smart moves with their identity: A) they shortened their name and B) they gave their signature more mass. 9. Nordstrom changed from their humanist font and increased the weight of their signature. 10. Both logo and signature of Fitbit are improved with more weight and with the logo and signature each being in a single color instead of two colors each. 11. The Recording Academy swapped its serif font for a heavier humanist font. They'll probably go straight sans serif before long.

12. Santander also traded in their serif font for a heavier sans serif. 13. Kemper replaced their gradient logo with a cleaner and heavier wordmark. 14. Experian increased their weight but will find the multi-color wrap-around logo ineffective. 15. Dale Carnegie's new identity looks more modern and credible. 16. Another identity with a more solid look. 17. RadioShack made its logo heavier and more compact. 18. Why did Dell minimize their good wordmark by putting it inside a circle? And now they've taken away even more mass. Two moves in the wrong direction.

Chapter 47

Deadly Sin of Logo Design #3 Fixed:

Having Enough Contrast

Contrast is Rooted in Value

Every color has a value. As mentioned in chapters 8, 39 and 40, the minimum contrast of a logo should not be lower than 40% and a signature's contrast should not be lower than 60% regardless of whether it is a positive or reversed identity.

A designer who only designs an identity for a light or white background has only done half a job. Every identity should be able to be reversed out of a dark background. For these situations, an alternate corporate color may be employed to assure enough contrast.

Yellows only work well on dark backgrounds, they do not give enough contrast on light or white backgrounds. Whatever motivates a designer to break this principle will evaporate to insignificance if the identity can not be easily seen. Yellows only can be used for very simple shapes.

Each of the above identities corrected signature contrasts that were too low.

The Tronc identity works well on white but fails on a black background. Alternate colors should have been used for the "n" and "c" for reversal situations.

Yellows as logo can only be used for very simple shapes, such as the Best Buy tag, the National Geographic logo or Synchrony logos. Shell's yellow would never show up well if it weren't for the containing red shape. Yellows can work for a background color as with IMDB but not for complex graphics like the Sprint logo (only equal to a 14% gray) or the Nikon logo. Sooner or later they will figure that out.

Chapter 48

Deadly Sin of Logo Design #4 Fixed:

Removing Wayward Parts

(Parts Out of Harmony)

The Problem with Badges

The biggest issue with a badge style logo is that the corporate name must be subordinated within a shape. In many respects, this is the same as Containment (Chapter 30).

A worse issue with badges is the tendency to wrap text around the shape, which significantly decreases the ease of reading it.

Through bitter experience, many companies have abandoned the badge approach in favor of a separate logo and "liberated" type, which also gives the options of having the text below, to the side and at different sizes to fit varying design constraints.

Harley-Davidson's badge logo is an exception because its type is legible, having kept the company name text flat and big enough to read with excellent contrast.

The Wrong Mood or Feeling

Designers must cultivate the ability to see how their creations will be perceived by the client's customers. Even if the concept of the logo is Corporate Activity, Corporate Name or even Abstract, the manner in which it is executed needs to feel harmonious with the corporate ideals.

There are many subtleties that come into play in identity design. Shapes and fonts carry stylistic subliminal messages that must be appropriate for your client.

In most of the samples shown here, a more appropriate mood is achieved for the company in question. One identity might look too casual and not formal enough, while another might look too strait-laced and "corporate," lacking refinement. It depends on the client's needs and the desired perception on the part of the client's customers.

1. Peace Coffee's multi-color badge had sloppier type; its new signature is easier to read while keeping a hand-rendered look. 2. Highland Brewing's logo had too many elements, many of which are quite illegible. Their new one is improved a bit, but still has hard-to-read parts. 3. League of Legends has a separate logo now, but the words "League of Legends" is too small. 4. Clube Athletico Paranaense got rid of its badge but the CAP acronym is handicapped by letters with drop shadows that are too small for clar-

ity. 5. Stanley Park's badge had illegible microtype. It's new identity is much easier to read, although its containing shape is rather random. 6. Juventus has a recognizable monogram now but insists on keeping their name small, a mistake. 7. Right to Dream had very abused type. Their clean logo and type are a huge improvement. 8. Starbucks is one of the few companies on the planet that can forego having a signature at all. Even though their badge was one of the cleanest and easiest to read, they saw the ben-

efit of converting it to a logo without the wrap-around type. 9. There is no denying the longevity of the Harley-Davidson badge logo. If only all badges could be as clean. 10. You probably don't know who ACM are from just their identity (fail!). They are A.C. Milan, a popular European soccer team. They not only need a separate signature but a corporate activity phrase as well. 11. Cardinal Stage had a much more legible identity that they swapped for this cryptic badge with type that is too thin for clarity.

1. Infotech had a sloppy check mark logo, a bad quality for a technology company. Now they have a new company name and new brand. 2. Hilton's old logo looked like a poor 1950s design as did its unkerned signature; their changes are appropriate for a higher class hotel chain. 3. Just redrawing their script wordmark with uniform stroke thickness, Lilly made themselves look more contemporary. 4. Frontier's old logo joined a serif italic "f" with a mostly sans serif wordmark, topped off with a hackneyed swoosh. The new identity is so much better. 5. Khan Academy's logo looked a little too casual and juvenile; the new one is more credible. 6. The Philbrook Museum of Art logo was meaningless shapes in a rectangle, a poor association for an institution that tries to combat the notion that modern art is meaningless. Their new mongram is a person looking at something, the experience they provide. 7. Lendingtree's signature used a dated looking font; they fixed it along with a stylish logo. 8. Pinterest switched its signature to look more business-like. A good move. 9. NASA's 1958 logo had a hokey old "Star Trek" feeling. In 1975 they switched to the "worm" monogram, but switched back to the retro looking "meatball" in 1992. In 2020 NASA came to its senses and went back to the 1975 monogram. Because it conforms to the core principles it can serve NASA indefinitely. 10. Sotheby's sans serif signature may have looked a little too corporate and so they switched to a serif font. 11. Instagram shifted from a more random script to a more uniform script, making it more business-like. 12. Epcot changed its hodgepodge signature to a more futuristic wordmark, in keeping with their theme. 13. The former Dallas Convention and Visitors Bureau wordmark looked casual and they changed it to have a more business oriented look. 14. Alberta changed their 90s feeling wordmark to a more casual look. 15. Logitech's old logo was very casual, the wrong mood for a technology company; the new wordmark with it's innovative "g" is much more appropriate. 16. The Bookman font was very popular in the 60s and 70s, but now looks dated. Michaels new hand-rendered script wordmark is more contemporary and more feminine, as are the majority of their customers. 17. News Corporation had a weak serif for its signature but the handwritten look of their new wordmark does not look precise or authoritative. 18. Boston.com's former wordmark looked too playful, even juvenile. The newer one looks more appropriate for business. 19. Destination America's hand painted backgrounds verge on the sloppy; the new ones look cleaner without looking too corporate. 20. DeviantArt's logo had dated 80's looking letters. The new one is very contemporary. 21. A data technology agency, Essence is much better served by its new wordmark than by its old one.

Chapter 49

Deadly Sin of Logo Design #5 Fixed:

Having No Overlapping Elements

Shadows or Outlines on Signatures
Even when drop shadows are done properly, they generally do not make for easier reading, as there is more for the eye take in. Sooner or later, clients will realize this and want cleaner, easier-to-read type in their identities.

1. The Campbell's script wordmark was designed clear back in 1869. It has served them well. Then in the 1990s someone decided to give it a black drop shadow, no doubt, to "boost legibility." It did not last long as they saw that legibility was lessened, not improved. **2.** Hershey's use of dimensional type on its labels is another example of someone's "good" idea that turns out to be bad. **3.** The Hertz heavy drop shadow was an attempt to make yellow have contrast against black. The yellow bar underneath the new signature is much better. **4.** Hobby Lobby's orange type with white halo plus a blue border and shadow made a very complex signature. Their simpler signature is so much easier to read. **5.** Even with Little Caesar's much smaller black signature compared to the outlined orange one, it is easy to see which gives the greater clarity.

1. Avianca | **Avianca**

2. dish NETWORK | **dish**

3. ebay | **ebay**

4. StaDt Wien | **Stadt Wien**

5. tresorit | **tresorit**

6. You Tube | **YouTube**

1. Avianca's abstract wavy lines were not a major nuisance, but the signature is more readable without them and their logo is recognizeable. 2. Dish Network's original identity was created in 1996. Since then, they have altered their identity six times, usually omitting elements that were finally seen as unnecessary. Six times in twenty three years is some sort of record and must have taken a financial toll. 3. Ebay's mishmash of lower case with caps and different fonts plus different colors has given way to one font, all in lower case. The multi-colored treatment is still used, but a single color version is also used. 4. Vienna's Stadt Wien with its hodgepodge of caps and lowercase as well as different fonts was interrupted with the shield. Now the shield is a focal point and the type can be easily read. 5. Tresorit's former logo comes across as a hexagon with a two-toned stripe that was actually supposed to be an isometric black cube with a stripe. It didn't reproduce well. Their new logo, with a gradient can also be shown in a single solid color. 6. YouTube's famous TV screen icon has been removed from the wordmark and replaced with a separate logo.

1. ALCOA | **Alcoa**

2. BEST BUY | **BEST BUY.**

3. Boots | **Boots**

4. Eventbrite | **Eventbrite**

5. JCPenney | **JCPenney**

6. MasterCard | **mastercard**

7. Principal Financial Group | **Principal**

8. Kashi | **Kashi**

9. Snapple | **Snapple**

10. Zillow | **Zillow**

11. Rexall | **Rexall**

12. WNBA | **WNBA**

1. The original Alcoa logo was solid but is improved by being brought outside the containing shape. 2. Best Buy's former signature was always subordinated to the price tag shape; now it is freed and the price tag is subordinate to it, as it should be. 3. The oval around the Boots signature added some mass, but little else. Now the wordmark has undergone a few modest changes and can be bigger in the same space. 4. Eventbrite's signature can also be bigger in the same space without the containing shape. 5. JCPenney's signature was dwarfed inside that square. Now it is free. 6. MasterCard's identity is cleaner with the signature separated from the logo. 7. Principal got rid of its containing triangle, which took a lot of space, and replaced it with a logo. 8. Kashi omitted its flag shape, which didn't match it's straight type, and is much more effective. 9. Snapple straightened its type and took it out of the red racetrack shape for a cleaner identity. 10. Zillow decided that the house shape was already a container for their stylized "Z" monogram, so why have another container around that? Besides, the former logo could remind someone of a house being swept away in a tornado. Getting rid of that was also a smart move. 11. Rexall's heavier wordmark is a big improvement over its former tightly contained identity. 12. WNBA's monogram was so tiny inside its containment that it was often illegible. This redesign is a major improvement.

Chapter 50

Deadly Sin of Logo Design #6 Fixed:

Making More Refined Shapes

Design Implies Shape

The very word design implies shapes that have been made with deliberation. When it comes to identity design, that often means simplifying, getting things down to the essence or more refined shapes. This usually results in a more recognizable image, which is exactly what good identity design is all about.

In the samples shown, it is not always about going from a poor identity to a good one. Sometimes this is about incremental improvements and subtle refinement, as in the case of the Kellogg's wordmark. In other examples, refinement has giving better visual clarity with simpler and more elegant shapes. When it comes to many small shapes, it reenforces how less is more and bigger is better.

1. Most people would never notice the several subtle changes to the Kellogg's wordmark, but they are there. It was already good; now it's a bit more solid. 2. Twitter now feels they are well known enough to omit their signature and just go with their new and improved logo. As with many new logos, it is entirely created with repeated shapes: circles and circle arcs. 3. Intel's former logo had a dropped "e" ligature that seemed somewhat forced. While not overly inspired, the new identity is still an improvement. 4. Ball State University already had a nicely designed logo. It has been further refined with simpler and slightly larger negative shapes and wisely cropped their figure to only show the most interesting part. The sans serif signature is also easier to read. 5. Ontario Volleyball's new identity synthesizes the best part of its former version into an elegant symbol. They also got rid of the wrap-around type, a legibility nightmare. 6. State Street's clipper ship woodcut logo was too complex and filled in when printed small or when viewed online in pixels. Its new, simpler variation is so much better. 7. The new American Express soldier does the same and reproduces better on the printed page and on any electronic screen.

Chapter 51

Deadly Sin of Logo Design #7 Fixed:

Omitting Thin Lines or Tiny Shapes

Thin Shapes Don't Reproduce Well

Fine lines and thin shapes have a tendency to fill in when printed in reverse. This happens in almost every kind of printing: offset, letterpress, silk screen and even ink jet. The problem happens on coated stock but will be even worse on uncoated paper. Even positive lines that are thin present difficulties in certain kinds of printing. And sooner or later a client will need to or want to reverse their identity.

Online imagery is viewed through a grid of pixels. If the shapes are too thin, they will not occupy a whole pixel and will be reproduced in a color that is somewhere between the image color and the background color. Too many of these small shapes result in "pixel mush."

There's no getting away from it: fine lines and thin shapes will cause problems and should be avoided in identity design.

1. Bank of America opened up the spaces in their logo. Unfortunately, they also switched their signature to all caps and allowed too much letterspacing, resulting in it looking smaller and less legible compared to the previous one. **2.** Dominion Energy replaced their too-fine light rays emanating from a fingertip with a solid "D" monogram with spaces thick enough to not fill in. **3.** General Electric has had virtually the same identity since 1909 but in 2004 they thickened their lines a bit to prevent the difficulties we've been talking about. **4.** Northeast Utilities changed their name to Eversource. They could have fixed the logo with fewer wedges and more space between them but Eversource opted for a wordmark with a multicolored logo (not good) in the middle of their wordmark (also not good). We can expect they will change it again in a few years to fix these mistakes.

5. State Farm stubbornly kept the words in the middle of their three ovals long after they were no longer legible. Finally, they omitted the containment square and maintained their three ovals without words. **6.** Gap had problems with their thick and thin Didone family font in the square because it kept filling in. They replaced it with a heavyweight font with an overlapped gradient square. After only six years they went back to their previous font but in positive. It will still give them problems. **7.** The Historic Houses Association has replaced their logo with a sturdier logo that communicates "historic" and "houses" much better. They also got rid of their HHA acronym and replaced their serif font with a sans serif font. **8.** Yum! made a solid change by replacing their thick-thin serif font with a slab serif. **9.** Going heavier in the font

is not always the answer. Intuit had a wordmark with a solid, heavy font, but the spaces between letters was so tight that they tended to fill in. They could have opened up their word mark but they opted for a new design with a medium weight font. **10.** Papa Johns had a similar problem with their heavy slab serif font; the spaces between letters were too tight. They changed it to a similar weight sans serif that is more readable. **11.** The negative spaces in the Rogers logo were too tight. They lightened the elements and opened the spaces a bit. We will see if they opened the spaces enough. **12.** Kijiji is an online classified seller. When you have a company name that is difficult to read, it is best to have as simple a font as possible. Kijiji kept their playful feeling while making their wordmark much cleaner.

Chapter 52

Good Trends in 21st Century Identity Design

Losing a Weak Logo

In recent times some companies have omitted logos from their identities. In fairness, most of those logos were weak, violating one or more of the Seven deadly Sins of Logo Design. But, as mentioned in Chapter 14, an identity consisting of a signature alone usually only works for consumer brand products like Gillette, Alka-Seltzer and Hertz Rent-a-Car, etc. Only a few of the samples here are such businesses. For most of them, a better approach would have been to redesign their logos. Plain signatures are inherently weaker than a good logo with a signature or a wordmark.

In spite of these examples, losing the logo is not a trend in 21st century identity design. Instead, as we have seen in the preceding several chapters, companies and their designers are feeling their way toward the principles that are the foundation of this book.

That ought to tell you something.

1.-4. Charter Communications, Cognizant, First Data and Scotiabank all got rid of their problematic logos which were, admittedly, weak. But the end result in each case is less personality in their identities. 5. Halliburton's logo was ill proportioned, the logo was too big in relation to the signature and the H was too small in relation to the circle. But otherwise, it was a decent logo. The worst part of the identity was the use of an extended font for an already long signature. Unbelievably, that is the only part they kept. Throw away the better part and keep the weaker part. What were they thinking? 6. Losing a logo isn't always a bad idea. Dunkin' Donuts shortened its name and its identity to Dunkin' alone. Removing the logo was no big loss as it wasn't very memorable. They kept the very appropriate font and the net result was quite positive. 7. SanDisk threw away their logo, which was somewhat uninspired and had very thin positive and negative lines. They also switched to a slab serif font to give the wordmark more mass. All in all, a good move for them. 8. Fuji Film finally got rid of its horrible logo and replaced its signature with a wordmark. Again, another change for the better. 9. Black & Decker's decision to change its identity is baffling. The logo was solid. The signature font had fairly small counters that might fill in at small sizes, so it could have been replaced with another sturdy font with counters that were a bit more open. The ampersand did not fit the rest of the type and also needed to be replaced, but overall it wasn't a bad identity. It had a feeling of strength that could have served them well with some adjustments. When they changed to the new identity, they lost the sturdy look and added shallow containment for what can only be described as a much weaker identity.

A Move Away From Serif Fonts

When talking about thin shapes, we have concentrated on logos, but the same principles apply to the fonts used for the signatures or wordmarks in identity design.

Serifs are, in most fonts, smaller and thinner than the strokes that make up their letterforms. Many companies have found these problematic. This is why so many brands are moving away from serifs in their signatures and wordmarks. If you go back through the last several chapters, you will see how many font changes have gone from serif to sans serif. The one part of the serif world that still is useful are the slab serifs, because the serifs tend to be sturdier.

As a practical experiment, go back through the chapters is this section and see how serif and humanist fonts have been abandoned in favor of san serif.

1. AIG left behind their serifs with their new sans serif identity. **2.** Stockholms Stad (the municipality of Stockholm, Sweden) replaced its wraparound serif type with straight sans serif that has a bit more weight. They also simplified their coat of arms to be one color. **3.** HSBC increased the size of their logo relative to their signature and compensated by using a clearer sans serif font with heavier weight. **4.** Reader's Digest joins the host of other companies abandoning their former serif wordmarks with a clean sans serif one. **5.** Travelers shortened their name as well as going to a sans serif font with a single color umbrella logo. **6.** Nvidia traded its two-color logo as well as its lower-uppercase mix and its regular and italic mix for a single color logo and with a sturdy sans serif signature.

Didone is Dead

A subset of serif fonts that are even more problematic are the Didone Family. They are represented by fonts such as Bodoni, Modern, Didot, etc. Because of their thick and thin strokes, especially in their serifs, they have long been avoided by identity designers with good reason. Those thin strokes fill in too often to be viable for branding design. For those few times where they have been used, the lifespan of those designs has been short, having been replaced by fonts that do not have such thick-thin properties. While fine for other uses, they are not suitable for identity design.

The Didone Family of Fonts

Members of the Didone family of fonts are perfectly suitable for many design applications, but corporate identity is not one of them. Why? Because they have such thin serifs and other thin strokes. Those tend to fill in when reversed or when seen at a distance. Many designers have tried to ignore this fact over the years and use them anyway, but none have succeeded. (Are you listening, GAP?)

Chapter 53

Famous Fails

In Recent Branding History

Some may think the Seven Deadly Sins of Logo Design in this book are just my arbitrary opinions, and as such, may be either accepted or easily dismissed. The whole purpose of this book has been to let you see with your own eyes that violating these principles can and will break an identity. We have seen that dozens, even hundreds of companies have paid incalculable sums over the years, some of them repeatedly, to fix their identities because *they just didn't work.*

If I don't know about the law of gravity and I trip, I will still fall. It never fails. If I accidentally back into a hot stove, I will get burned. And if I consume something toxic, it will do me harm and it won't matter that I didn't know.

Ignorance of **immutable laws** gives **no immunity** to the outcome of breaking them

Ignorance of immutable laws gives no immunity to the consequences of breaking them. A person who does not comprehend a principle will not avoid the outcome of breaking that principle.

You can run, but you can't hide from unalterable, bedrock principles. It doesn't matter whether you are a famous designer or a beginner; if your identity is guilty of one of the Deadly Sins of Logo Design, it won't work, at least not consistently.

Here are three examples of large, world-class corporations that changed their identities to new designs, identities that committed one or more of the Seven Deadly Sins of Logo Design and, as a result, their logos did not work.

After we have seen what these three companies did to their identities, we will also see in Chapter 54 that they each have abandoned their misguided logos.

AT&T

The excellent AT&T identity designed by Saul Bass was changed in 2005 after a corporate restructuring. Many identities have been replaced at such times, but not always for the better. The new AT&T design may have been been an homage to the original Bass logo, but it was a much weaker version of it.

As with so many designs that start from the 3-D color version instead of a plain, solid form, the shapes are less than esthetically refined. The design can't work when printed in a single flat color, which means that ALL printing for this company's identity must be in full color.

This is particularly noteworthy when vehicles and signage are considered. Instead of the more durable cut vinyl in solid colors, ALL vehicles and signage must be done in printed vinyl. It may look cool, but it only lasts about one third of the time of cut vinyl, meaning quicker replacement times. This is a massive extra expense for a company that has many thousands of vehicles in its fleet. Besides, the darkest parts of the new logo are barely a 40% value (minimal contrast), and most are much lighter, giving the overall logo poor contrast.

Also, changing the signature from all caps to all lower case letters makes it look insipid.

I am not privy to what AT&T paid to Interbrand to create this new identity, but you can be sure it was over six figures. Add to that the cost of implementing this identity, which must be in the millions of dollars. Even if you ignore the cost of rebranding their stationery, invoices, their employee uniforms and hardhats, just the cost to put this on the thousands of vehicles in their fleet and

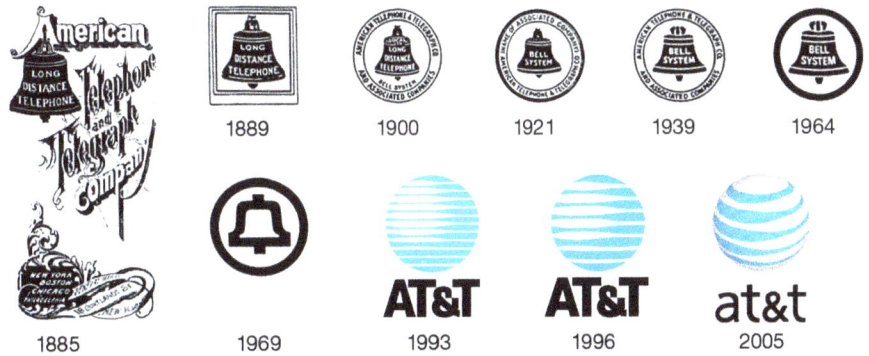

The progression of the AT&T identity with the Saul Bass logo in 1993, which was improved by him again in 1996. Then they adopted an inferior identity in 2005.

on every building they use would be a staggering sum. And all for a logo that doesn't work.

Here are the Deadly Sins of Logo Design committed in this new identity:
- Does not work in solid black.
- Unrefined shapes
- Poor contrast

Sounds like three strikes and you're out.

When you render the 2005 AT&T logo stripes in black you see the clumsy nature of some of those shapes. On vehicles and signage, the logo can not be made of solid color vinyl and has minimal contrast. After a few years, AT&T recognized the contrast issues of their logo and even refined some of the shapes a bit. Note that this slightly improved variation only works in reverse. It was a stop-gap measure and, apparently, did not have a positive version.

United Airlines

Saul Bass also designed excellent logos for United Airlines and Continental Airlines. They were classic logos that could have lasted forever, but Continental replaced its logo in 1991. Then in 2010 Continental began a merger with United Airlines, which was completed in 2012 with the new combined entity keeping United's name but Continental's logo. In effect, both airlines traded two superior logos for one inferior one.

The new Continental/United logo commits the deadly sin of too-small elements and lines. As a result, it doesn't reproduce well in a myriad of applications. The fine lines in the logo even get deformed when printed on the company's own boarding passes. How many thousands of passes are given to customers every day?

I flew on Continental during the last year they went by that name. The flight was OK. The seats had individual movie screens on the back for watching in-flight movies. Nice. But on the plane's start-up, for quite a while before the airline had any movies, they only showed the Continental identity. The screen was good enough for movies, but the logo's lines were so small there just weren't enough pixels for each line to be either pure white or pure blue. It looked horrible. Pixel mush.

You can be sure that Continental paid Lippincott & Marguiles a pretty penny to have its new logo designed. But that is just a drop in the bucket compared with the expense of implementing the new identity. When you consider the size of the graphics that go on airplanes alone, the cost to put the identity on every plane is shocking. And how

The different corporate identities of Continental Airlines.

The long history of United Airlines identity up to 2012.

many planes do the two combined airlines own? In addition, there are other vehicles, signage, and so much more. What a monstrous expenditure made to implement a broken logo.

Deadly Sin of Logo Design committed in this new identity:

• Lines too thin, elements too small

It only takes one hole to make a blowout.

The Continental Airlines identity as it appeared on the screens of the company's own plane seats. The logo parts are too small for individual pixels to be either the correct blue or white.

Xerox

When you think Xerox, you likely think photocopiers, right? Now the company has graduated to earning the bulk of its revenue in higher-end printers. It is particularly paradoxical, then, to see this 2007 identity from Xerox. Its fancy 3-D ball logo didn't print well.

Xerox paper comes in nice white cardboard cartons labelled with the new Xerox identity. Most printing on cardboard is done with Flexography (basically, a giant rubber stamp mounted on a drum). Look at the fine lines that crisscross in the middle of the logo **(A)**. Notice how deformed they are. Why? Because those lines are too fine to print properly from a raised rubber printing plate.

Inside each Xerox paper carton are several reams of photocopy paper, and each of those has a printed paper wrapper. The wrappers appear to be printed in letterpress so that the plates can hold up to the millions of wrappers printed. The logos are black and red **(B)**. In addition to the black being slightly out of register with the red–a reason to avoid two-color logos–the lines are blotchy, a function of the lines being so thin. Remember, this second example is not on crude cardboard as on the box, but on fine, semi-gloss paper. Still the reproduction is poor.

Lastly, when you go to use a Xerox printer, the machine has a color touchscreen control panel. But even here, on their own machine, the logo does not reproduce well **(C)**. The light gray crisscross lines in the middle are supposed to get lighter in the reflected light on the logo's spherical surface. But on the Xerox machine's own screen, the lines look totally bleached out.

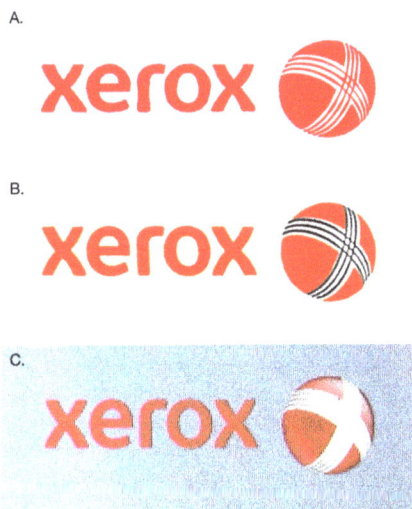

1906   1949   1954   1954   1957

1961   1968   1968   1994

2002   2004   2007

A.

B.

C.

How ironic to have a company whose bread and butter is printing reproduction with a logo that reproduces so poorly. Isn't that the definition of abject failure for whoever was involved in that identity design?

Deadly Sins of Logo Design committed in this new identity:
- Multiple colors in the logo
- Thin lines, tiny elements
- Poor contrast

Is There a Lesson Here?

These three examples of Famous Fails represent many millions of dollars wasted on inferior graphic design and the implementation of those designs.

The saddest thing is that there is no need for weak identities like this in the first place. The principles we've spoken of here are bedrock and immutable. They do not move aside for fad or fashion. They remain true whether you believe in them or not.

The good news is that these principles can be learned by anyone with the clarity of thought to recognize them and the discipline to practice them.

Superior design awaits.

Chapter 54

Correction at a Cost

When the first edition of this book was published, all three of the "Famous Fails" logos were still being used by their respective companies. Since then, they have all gotten rid of those broken logos.

AT&T Identity Fixed

Ten years after adopting their faulty 3-D corporate identity, and after their unsuccessful attempts to mend things by reversing the design out of solid cyan and orange, AT&T threw in the towel and had their identity reworked. Not only did they abandon the transparent globe look of the 2005 logo, they also left behind the impotent lower case at&t signature for the previous AT&T signature all in upper case. The stripes of the old logo were significantly reworked to much more esthetically pleasing shapes and now are shown in a solid cyan that has better contrast on a white background.

2005

2015

Here are the 2005 and 2015 AT&T logos superimposed over each other. The warmer two sets of colors are the newer shapes and the cooler two colors are the older shapes. While it is hard to appreciate the esthetics of the new shapes in this comparison, it does show that every single shape needed refinement to fix the old logo.

Consider the cost of such signage and vehicle graphics.

United Airlines Identity Fixed

The overly intricate logo adopted by Continental airlines and inherited by United airlines after the merger of the two companies was too complex for clean reproduction. United had to simplify it.

Given the fact that as of 2019, United Airlines owns a fleet of 767 huge aircraft, not to mention their hundreds of ground support vehicles, airport signage, and personnel, one can understand if they don't immediately redo all of that for brand consistency.

For our purposes, it is enough for them to attempt to correct a poor design that never should have been adopted in the first place.

The newer simpler United Airlines logo changed from ten longitude pairs to six, and from nine latitude lines down to six. The result is a logo that at least can survive on the company's own website and on the plane seat screens, unlike its predecessor.

Xerox Logo Abandoned

It took Xerox eleven years to realize that there was no way to fix the problems in their 3-D logo; it just wouldn't work. Their solution was to omit the logo from the identity altogether. The remaining signature is all lower case, but these particular letters do not evoke as much

The 2008 and 2019 versions of the Xerox corporate identity

of a sense of weakness as the former at&t lower case signature.

This identity overhaul may not sound as painful as the other Famous Fails, but implementing the change to their buildings and machines and packaging and products still represents a significant financial outlay.

Is There A Lesson Here?

Again, these three rebrandings were not without cost, but this was *not* wasted money. The money spent on the previous flawed identities, designed contrary to the Core Principles, was the wasted money.

To recap, any identity that violates one or more of the Seven Deadly Sins will not work. Sooner or later the client will realize this. And who will they go to for a brand revision? If I were the CEO of such a company, I would never go back to the designers that gave me the flawed identity that now needs to be replaced.

Chapter 55

Learning From the Past

You Can't Beat Success

When we look over the last century of branding design we see thousands upon thousands of companies that have each proudly worn their corporate identities. Virtually all of them have changed their identities, not just once, but many times. And at no small expense.

And yet some companies have not had that misfortune. Their identities have stood the test of time. Some for thirty, fifty, even a hundred years. If you will look closely, every one of them has avoided the Seven Deadly Sins of Logo Design.

Not committing any of these sins does not guarantee superb design, but committing any one of those sins does guarantee that such an identity will not work and will likely need to be replaced sooner or later. And as we have already stressed, such changes are attended by significant expenses that could otherwise have been avoided.

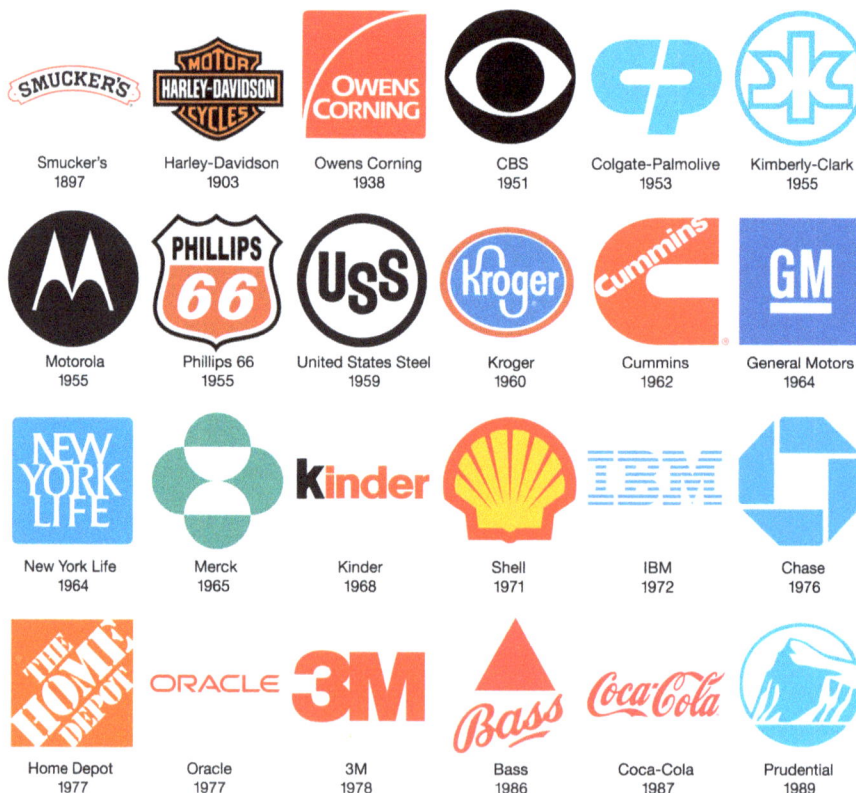

Smucker's 1897	Harley-Davidson 1903	Owens Corning 1938	CBS 1951	Colgate-Palmolive 1953	Kimberly-Clark 1955
Motorola 1955	Phillips 66 1955	United States Steel 1959	Kroger 1960	Cummins 1962	General Motors 1964
New York Life 1964	Merck 1965	Kinder 1968	Shell 1971	IBM 1972	Chase 1976
Home Depot 1977	Oracle 1977	3M 1978	Bass 1986	Coca-Cola 1987	Prudential 1989

These logos, monograms and wordmarks have survived a minimum of three decades. Some of them may not be designs that you would aspire to, but they have served their clients well and have not been crippled by any of the Seven Deadly Sins of Logo Design, and, therefore, have not needed to be replaced.

Whole Identity Aspect

In the preceding examples, can you see how much smaller the four wordmarks (Smuckers, Kinder, Oracle, Coca-Cola) are in a horizontally limited space like this grid? This is because of their overall aspect, which is their relative width versus height. Most words used for wordmarks will naturally have a wider-shorter aspect than most logos and, therefore, they will appear smaller in any situation where the horizontal space is limited, such as when the space is limited by columns: one column newspaper ads or Yellow Pages ads or even a company's own publications.

This is why there is a natural advantage to an identity consisting of a logo or monogram accompanied by a signature instead of a wordmark. With a wordmark, you only have one overall shape. With a logo or monogram plus a signature, there are different arrangements and size relationships that can maximize visibility in different design layouts, as seen in chapter 43.

Generally speaking, aspect will be harder to deal with when there are more letters in the functional corporate name. A name with four to eight letters is very comfortable to design with. Names with ten, twelve or more letters become increasingly difficult to manage.

As was mentioned in Chapter 42, one good way to compensate for long names is to use more condensed fonts.

The Rebranding of Caterpillar

Around 1989, Marshall Strategy was hired to do a major rebranding for Caterpillar, the heavy equipment manufacturer. Prior to this, Caterpillar had a serviceable (if not inspiring) logo but the long signature was made even shorter vertically relative to its width by using an extended font. Bad call.

In the new identity, Helvetica Condensed Bold was used to excellent effect, not only giving the signature more height relative to its width, but more mass as well. The incorporation of the yellow wedge does not interfere with legibility and reminds viewers of the corporate color used to paint all their equipment.

The shorter version of the identity to just "CAT" remains perfectly balanced with the wedge. Going with the shorter name recognizes the way most customers refer to them, similar to how Federal Express changed its functional name to FedEx.

Caterpillar's successful brand change is one of the rare times when trading a logo and signature for a wordmark was a smart move. However, trading a logo and signature for just a plain signature usually results in an overall weaker identity.

Top: The old Caterpillar logo and signature. **Middle and Bottom:** the new Caterpillar identity by Marshall Strategy. The new identity has so much more mass than the old one, a quality consistent with the kind of heavy equipment that they build. Abbreviating the name to just CAT is even better and will likely become the norm for them going forward.

Chapter 56

Responsive Websites, Avatars and Favicons

Responsive Websites

Many of us now do a significant amount of web searching on tablets and smart phones, not just our desktop or laptop computers. Hence the current pressure to have "responsive websites," sites that change the size and organization of a page's content, depending on the device used for viewing it.

Even though the resolution of these screens has increased, with more pixels per inch, the inescapable fact is that these screens are smaller. Therefore their content will be viewed smaller. One needs to think of this reality when designing an identity.

Social Media Avatars

Everyone knows how important social media is now, not just for individual people today, but for all sorts of companies as well. Facebook, Twitter, Pinterest and Instagram are the most popular, but the list goes on.

Social media allows the user to have an avatar, a visual portrait of the person—or for companies, their logo. An avatar can be nice and big on your own page in these sites, but the avatars on your notices, tweets or posts going to followers are quite small. As of this writing, here are the typical sizes of the big four social media for their avatar sizes for posts or tweets:

Twitter	42 pixels square
Pinterest	40 pixels square
FaceBook	32 pixels square
Instagram	30 pixels round

Obviously, clear and simple logos survive best in this social media arena. Logos without any of the Seven Deadly Sins are essential with such a limited number of pixels.

Avatars from Instagram posts on an iPhone. The top three rows are successful. The bottom row avatars all suffer from not recognizing the size that they must be viewed on posts. Utah Jazz's poor logo does not improve when reduced. Lippincott's avatar shows the problem not using a condensed font for long signatures and of using all caps. Calvin Klein's identity should be flexible enough to let the words to be stacked, which would have given critical size. Godiva doesn't understand that making things smaller than they need to be doesn't work for avatars. Real Canadian Superstore could have stacked its logo and signature or even used its logo alone for greater clarity. Mitsubishi's logo works well at this small size but the signature is marginal and the accompanying type is illegible and should have been omitted. Faces used as avatars are best close-cropped, and even then, are often only recognizable to people who already know the person.

Favicons

We'll end our journey with the humble little favicon (*fav* rhymes with *have*), short for favorite icon. These tiny nuggets of branding design can (and should) be part of every commercial website. When we visit any website that has a favicon, it will appear at the top of the browser window or tab of most browsers. Then, if we bookmark a web page, that site's favicon is stored along with the link and the bookmark's descriptive text. When we scroll through our web bookmarks, the favicon is the first thing we see, followed by the descriptive text.

How cool is that? You get to plant your favicon brand on the machine of anyone who bookmarks your site. The only problem is that these little visuals are only sixteen or thirty-two pixels square. That's not much to work with. And only logos free of the Seven Deadly Sins have any hope of converting directly to a clear little favicon.

The ideal favicon would be a miniature of the company's logo, like those for ABC, Microsoft, Facebook and Apple. The next best thing is an important portion of the logo, or the first initial of the company wordmark or signature, like those for Google, Bing or Amazon.

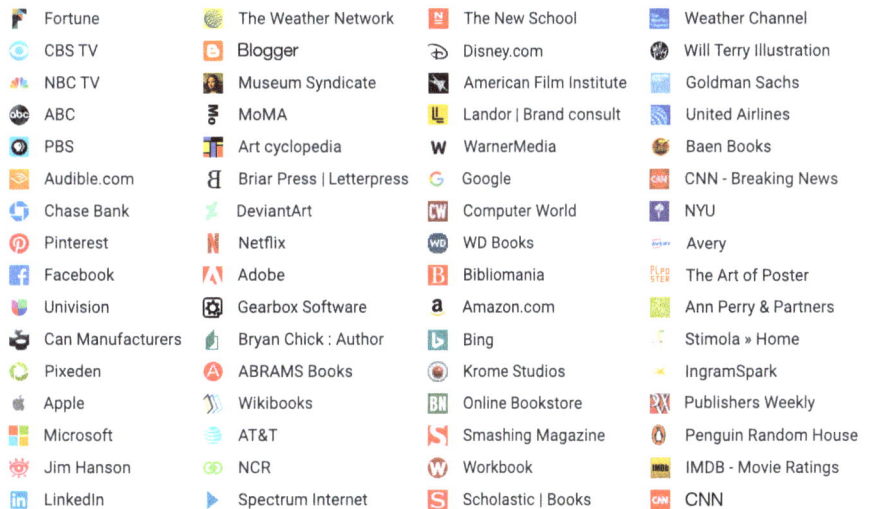

Fortune	The Weather Network	The New School	Weather Channel
CBS TV	Blogger	Disney.com	Will Terry Illustration
NBC TV	Museum Syndicate	American Film Institute	Goldman Sachs
ABC	MoMA	Landor | Brand consult	United Airlines
PBS	Art cyclopedia	WarnerMedia	Baen Books
Audible.com	Briar Press | Letterpress	Google	CNN - Breaking News
Chase Bank	DeviantArt	Computer World	NYU
Pinterest	Netflix	WD Books	Avery
Facebook	Adobe	Bibliomania	The Art of Poster
Univision	Gearbox Software	Amazon.com	Ann Perry & Partners
Can Manufacturers	Bryan Chick : Author	Bing	Stimola » Home
Pixeden	ABRAMS Books	Krome Studios	IngramSpark
Apple	Wikibooks	Online Bookstore	Publishers Weekly
Microsoft	AT&T	Smashing Magazine	Penguin Random House
Jim Hanson	NCR	Workbook	IMDB - Movie Ratings
LinkedIn	Spectrum Internet	Scholastic | Books	CNN

Favicons appear with our saved web bookmarks and are powerful little bits of marketing, only 16 or 32 pixels square. **Columns 1 and 2** are miniature versions of their very effective logos. **Column 3** shows favicons derived from a part of their identity. Companies that only use a signature end up having to make, in effect, a micro-logo for their favicon. **Column 4** are ineffective favicons for various reasons. The first are trying to show something too complex for a so fw pixels. Others have weak contrast.

It's nearly impossible to make a good favicon from a poor logo. Parts or lines that are too fine, lack mass or contrast are all accentuated when trying to shrink the logo down to 16 pixels square. What are a company's options then?

Not using a favicon at all?

Or, admitting total defeat, adopting a totally new micro logo that has no resemblance to the original identity?

Who would want to do that?

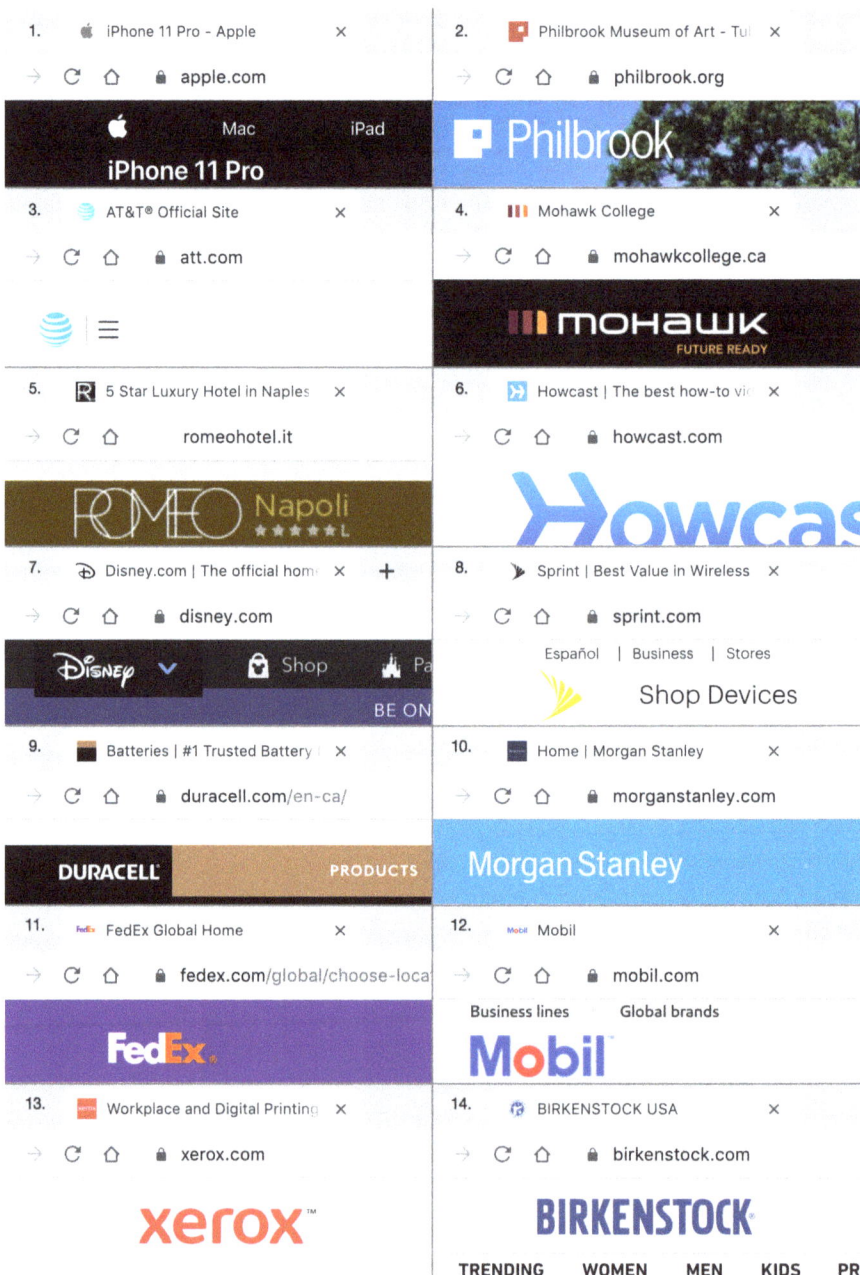

Here are the web browser tabs, URLs and identities of fourteen companies, right off their own websites, pixel for pixel. 1.-4. have good, solid logos that, in turn, make good, solid favicons. 5.-7. use a recognizable part of their identities, a reasonable alternative to the whole identity. 8. changed the favicon color to black to give better contrast. Their yellow logo also needs better contrast. 9. used the solid colors associated with their brand to good effect. 10. used their whole 13 letter signature without even stacking it to allow it to be bigger. It's completely unreadable. 11.-12. use their whole wordmarks but they are only five letters long each, which is the outside limit for a favicon. 13. should have done the same thing as 11 & 12 instead of a reversal in a solid block. It cost them some legibility. 14. Birkenstock used a visual both unrelated to its identity and so complex as to be quite illegible. What kind of logic is that?

Less is More

This is an age-old maxim in so many areas of art and design, as has already been mentioned. It is not just a nice idea in favicon design, it is imperative.

The websites for Kentucky Fried Chicken in the US and in Canada give us an opportunity to compare favicons. Both the US and Canadian favicons show the familiar bucket. The US version also tries to show the bucket full of chicken, whereas the Canadian version only shows the bucket flat on. It is very easy to tell that the simpler subject works better. Note that it only takes a few pixels to render the chicken, but it is enough to make the rest of the bucket considerably less clear.

The lesson?

In favicon design, reaching for less can make it better.

What Do 16 Pixel Images Teach Us?

One might suppose that the latest modern fads and fashions of logo design would be most compatible with our latest technology and media. But the opposite is true. Over and over we see that the Core Principles of logo design we've spoken of in this book are not only valid today, but give better results with today's newest media. What could be more modern than a favicon?

Far from being passé or old-fashioned, these principles are fundamental, even timeless. As we've stated before, trends are temporary and, in the end, will be replaced. That is the very meaning of the word trend, isn't it? So avoid trends—especially just the outward trappings of trends—at all costs.

Instead, let us seek in our corporate identity design that which aspires, at least, to permanence.

Chapter 57

Working at Creativity

Can Creativity be Cultivated?

Albert Einstein is not remembered for his graphic design, but he was responsible for an abundance of creative new ideas in the field of physics. Not all creativity is visual. Or musical. Or literary. Every area of human endeavor has the potential for creativity. Read what Einstein said about solving creative problems: "As one grows older, one sees the impossibility of imposing your will on the chaos with brute force. But if you are patient, there may come that moment when, while eating an apple, the solution presents itself politely and says, 'Here I am!'"

To be sure, it is wonderful to have an inspired idea occur to you. It feels like magic. And if the idea really was inspired, it can work like magic, too.

How do those moments happen? I don't know. But I do know how to encourage them to happen more often.

One way is to get engaged, really, deeply invested in your creative project as *early* as you can. Puzzle over the

issue. Be hard on yourself, and don't settle for a mediocre solution.

Then put the problem aside. Let your subconscious work on it for a while. Come back to it and slave on it again. Then put it aside again or sleep on it. I can't tell you how often a beautiful solution has presented itself to me in a dream or when working on something completely different. The answer just percolates to the surface unbidden, as Einstein suggested. Most often, such inspirations really do work well.

But if you are a procrastinator, someone who gets to a job at the last possible moment, you can forget about "percolation time." To summon that kind of help, you have to get the subconscious truly engaged. Once that has been done, your subconscious will work on your issue while you turn your conscious attention to something else. The key is that you have to give your subconscious time. If you don't, it doesn't have a chance to come up with those breakthroughs.

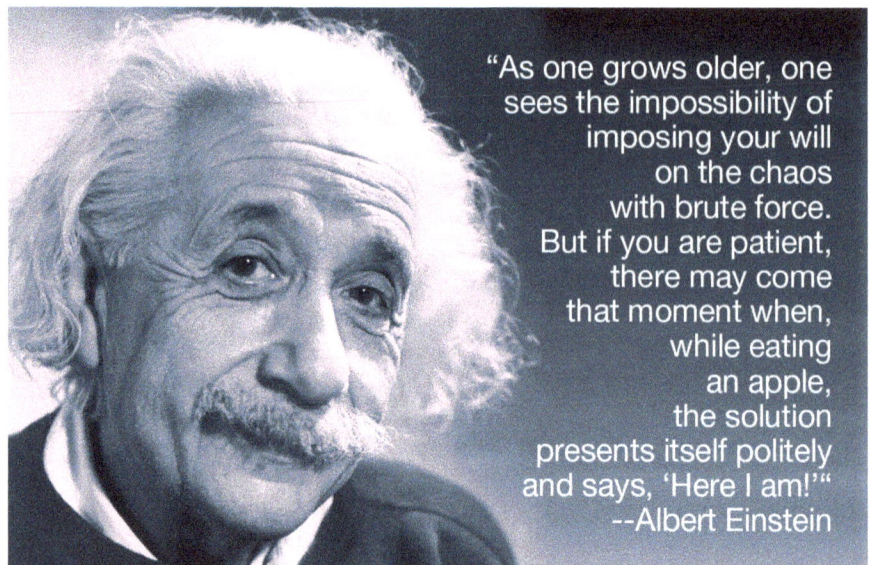

> "As one grows older, one sees the impossibility of imposing your will on the chaos with brute force. But if you are patient, there may come that moment when, while eating an apple, the solution presents itself politely and says, 'Here I am!'"
> --Albert Einstein

You might think that Einstein was saying that you can't influence the process of getting inspiration, but if you know anything about how he worked, you will see that he was advocating the method I've just explained.

Here's another key principle: don't simply sit and wait for inspiration to strike. Leonardo da Vinci said: "It has long since come to my attention that people of accomplishment rarely sat back and let things happen to them. They went out and happened to things."

Why do I bring this up?

Because those who fail to be proactive are artistic dilettantes, dabblers, pretenders.

Chuck Close is a celebrated photographic-realist painter. He was born with prosopagnosia, a brain defect that leaves him unable to recognize faces. Paradoxically, he made a successful career painting giant, ultra-realistic portraits. In 1988, he suffered a spinal artery collapse that left him almost totally paralyzed. Most people would have given up painting at that point, but he did not. Since then, he has continued to create giant portraits. Because his finer motor skills have been ruined by the paralysis, he breaks his portraits into large, multicolored boxes, each presenting an overall color.

Chuck Close's triumph over such obstacles lends weight to his famous quote: "Inspiration is for amateurs — the rest of us just show up and get to work."

Some people imagine that creativity is a mystical phenomenon that can't be promoted or consciously influenced. I beg to differ (and apparently, so do Einstein, da Vinci and Chuck Close).

"It has long since come to my attention that people of accomplishment rarely sat back and let things happen to them. They went out and happened to things."
--Leonardo da Vinci

"Inspiration is for amateurs— the rest of us just show up and get to work."
--Chuck Close

You have the power to summon the muse by your own actions. How do you increase the "eureka! moments"?

One way is to stimulate as much of your brain as soon as possible.

159

Working The System

The system I have already explained does exactly this. In relation to corporate identity design, we could make a checklist like this:

- Interview your clients.
- Discover specifically what they do
- Learn how they differ from their competitors
- Consider how their product or service might be represented simply
- Find out what their product or service does for their customers
- Discuss the ideals that they want associated with their company
- Discover what associations they most want to avoid
- Look up the meanings of their names (if any)

Sketch at least two concepts for each of the following combinations:

- Wordmarks showing corporate activity
- Monograms showing corporate activity
- Logos showing corporate activity
- Wordmarks with corporate ideals
- Monograms with corporate ideals
- Logos with corporate ideals
- Wordmarks showing the corporate name
- Monogram showing the corporate name
- Logos showing the corporate name
- Wordmarks using an abstract approach
- Monograms using an abstract approach
- Logos using an abstract approach

(This should give you a minimum of twenty-four concept sketches.)

Consider how each concept might be rendered with each of these visual processing techniques (even the weak, lame, stupid concepts):

- Meaningful Containment
- Planar or Silhouette
- Fragmentation
- Unique Coincidence
- Linear Treatment
- Ligatures and Flourishes
- Negative Shapes
- Essence
- System of Shapes
- Sculpted Type

Before executing any final designs, ensure that all seven deadly sins of logo design are avoided:

- Can't work in solid Black
- Lack of Mass
- Obscure contrast
- Wayward or disharmonious parts
- Overlapping elements
- Unrefined shapes
- Tiny elements, Thin lines

Can you even imagine that this process won't produce results superior to whatever haphazard method you could otherwise employ?

This method works.

But there's one catch:
YOU have to work at it.

No One Wants to be a Wannabe

I once listened to a podcast in which a woman had given a lecture on book publicity (a subject on which she was an expert) to a group of self-publishers. After the lecture, a lawyer asked how he might get publicity for his book. The woman was taken aback, because that was precisely the subject of her whole lecture: pre-publication reviews, ongoing reviews in all the media, radio interviews, book distribution and so on. She tried to recap these principles for the lawyer, but he brushed her explanation aside and again asked the same question. Apparently the lawyer thought that, because he was established in his own profession, he somehow could jump the queue in the business of publishing.

To me, that's what a wannabe is: someone who thinks he or she can arrive at the top of the mountain without climbing it. The helicopter ride to the summit may work for rich ski bums on physical mountains, but not in the real world in any career. Wannabes are amateur dabblers who won't submit to the discipline of the art form, but still think they can make it as professionals.

Wannabes are different from hobbyists who are practicing an art for their own enjoyment. They are also different from beginners who are committed to learning their craft. Every proficient designer was once a fledgling, even an "aspiring designer." There is no shame in that.

On the other hand, wannabes are guilty of the pride that makes them feel that they are special and are somehow exempt from the law of "paying your dues."

Equally absurd are those who think they have nothing to learn. I fully expect to learn many things from you, dear reader, by sharing this book. If I didn't, I'd assume I already knew it all. And I don't. But I have learned a few things, and I think others would like to learn them, too. Or at least consider them.

One of the differences between pursuing graphic design and working at another trade like plumbing is that we will never know it all. That, indeed, can be one of the joys of our profession—why it never gets old. So we are all learning, no matter at what stage we are in our career. And if we are legitimately always improving our craft, then we don't deserve the label of wannabe.

Chapter 58

Final Words

Four color process printing (CMYK) has been around for well over a century. Today many homes have their own color printers using the same color inks. Books, magazines and other printed materials are all about us, created with the true primary colors, cyan, magenta, and yellow, plus black.

Yet it is amazing that people are still being taught that red, yellow and blue are the primary colors. Not just in the homes of illiterate persons, but in the art programs of respected post-secondary institutions.

At least half of the books in print explaining color to artists continue to spread this misinformation, in spite of the fact that every one of those books are printed with magenta, yellow and cyan instead of red, yellow and blue. The majority of adults today were taught the "false primaries" in kindergarten. With few exceptions, the majority of kindergarten kids today are still being taught this false tradition.

It is incomprehensible to me that people refuse to give up concepts that clearly don't work.

I often explain to friends that the real primary colors are not red, yellow and blue, but rather magenta, yellow and cyan. When I can, I show them a true color wheel with magenta, yellow and cyan along with red, green and blue.

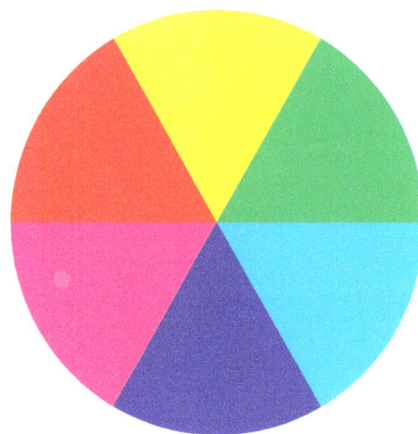

I point out that printed blue is a combination of magenta and cyan inks. I prove to their own eyes that printed red is a combination of magenta and yellow inks. This means that red is *not* a primary color because it is made up of two other colors. Even then, some will say something like, "But I *like* red better than magenta."

I answer, "It doesn't matter what you like. Red isn't a primary color. It can't be a primary if you can make it from two other colors."

Sometimes I change tactics and ask them to remember how they were told as children that red and blue would make purple. But when they tried it with their crayons, red and blue *did not* make purple, but just a muddy purplish color. That is because the red

already has yellow in it–a color far from purple. Neither did yellow and blue crayons make green. That is because blue already has magenta in it, a color opposite to green.

For some, their deep-seated guilt that they couldn't get the primary colors to work for them is erased. They know that it was because what they had been told about primary colors was wrong. It wasn't their fault that the crayons didn't work for them after all. This knowledge was a near miraculous insight, a breakthrough, an epiphany.

For a few others, they just could not accept what I told them about magenta, yellow and cyan. They had been brainwashed and couldn't get past their decades of conditioning that red, yellow and blue were the primary colors.

I have even seen art books on color that show two different color wheels: one labeled "The Scientific Color Wheel" (with the true primaries shown) and the other labeled "The Artists' Color Wheel" (with the false primaries shown).

Oh, really? Does the physics of light work differently for artists?

No.

Light and color only work one way. It is the epitome of ignorance to think a certain group of people can have physics work differently for them.

So it is with the Seven Deadly Sins of Logo Design. The reason why some things don't work is rooted in physics also, from the way our vision works to the nature of our printing methods. These are physical facts and ignoring them won't make them go away. These things aren't so because I say so. They just are. All I have done is put in the time to discover them.

Hopefully, the thousands of examples in this book have helped you see the truth about these Core Principles.

You have a choice to make. You can decide that these things are nice but you are going to continue to do your branding design as you have always done it. For most, that means hit and miss with their identity designs. Some work. Some don't.

Or you can decide to really dig in and see if these precepts are merely nice ideas or genuine principles that truly are immutable. Especially with the Seven Deadly Sins, if you violate even one of them, the identity you design will not work in some way that an identity ought to work.

Since design is not an exact science, but an art, by abiding by these principles, you will not be taking the joy out of creating, but rather, taking a short cut to more effective and better identity design.

Read these things again. Review them every time you do a new identity. Before long they will become a liberating path that will give your identities a more promising future.

A Shift in the Industry
I am not the proverbial voice crying in the wilderness. Many designers and companies are beginning to see that too often the "new trends" in logo design just don't work—or at least they don't work in enough situations where an identity *should* work. Hence, hundreds of logo redesigns have been made to correct their former flaws.

The cost of redesigning a corporate identity can be significant. But that is nothing compared to implementing the redesign throughout a company's website, stationery, signage, business forms, vehicles and so much more. For a small or mid-sized company the expenditure can be in the thousands or tens of thousands of dollars; for a large company it will surely be in the hundreds of thousands or even millions of dollars.

So many companies are realizing that their existing logos don't work like they should. These business owners don't know about the Seven Deadly Sins of Logo Design. But over time, they still see the effects of them, and are willing to pay to get rid of them.

It doesn't matter where knowledge comes from; when we find true principles, we would do well to adopt them.

To those who see the validity of what I've presented in this book, I say, it's not enough to accept it. Any art form requires practice and discipline. But be assured: practice and discipline, over time, bring mastery. There is no need to grope one's way blindly. Even so, the labor of branding design is labor indeed.

And when your branding design works, it doesn't just feel great, you may have created something that will touch thousands of lives and be useful for decades, maybe even forever.

Appendix 1: Glossary

Bitmap - a pixel based image, such as a photograph or image created in Photoshop, as opposed to vector based imagery.

CA Phrase - (see Corporate Activity Phrase)

Contrast - A difference in value between visual elements that determines legibility.

Contrast Differential - The percent of the difference in value between an element and its background.

Contrast, Excellent - 60% difference between the value of type and its background

Contrast, Minimum - 40% difference between the value of type or a logo and its background

Core Principles - Principles which do not change with fad or fashion, fundamental truths of identity design. Also called bedrock principles, immutable principles.

Corporate Activity Phrase - A word or words that concisely describes what a company does. This CA Phrase is added to a corporate identity for use in all out-of-context situations like signage, vehicles and also sometimes on business cards and advertising.

Counters - The negative or internal spaces in letterforms.

Creativity - The ability to solve problems

Curvilinear - Consisting of or bounded by curved lines.

Favicons - Small 16 (or 32) pixel square identifiers that are seen in some internet browsers tabs, in the address bar or in a list of saved bookmarks.

Flourishes - A decorative addition to typography that should not interfere with a word's core letterforms.

Functional Name - The name by which a company is commonly known, usually not including such legal endings as inc., incorporated, corporation or company, unless that is how the name is commonly used by customers.

Golden Mean, Golden Section - A proportion, roughly 1 to 1.666, discovered by Greek geometricians and which also appears frequently in nature; they considered it a divine proportion.

Halftone - Tiny dots that simulate grays when used together to break down a photographic image for printing.

Hue - The difference between colors in the rainbow or in the spectrum, as red is a different hue from orange or yellow.

Internal Contrast - The 40% minimum value difference between elements in an identity that allows for easy recognition of those elements.

Japanese Kamon - A logo-like symbol historically used in Japanese families to identify themselves.

Kerning - The act of adjusting the horizontal spaces between letters in larger type to make the words look more visually cohesive, called tracking in most software programs.

Law of Thirds - A principle that proposes that an image composition will be more dynamically balanced if dominant elements are placed at roughly one third/two thirds points in a picture plane.

Legibility - When visual elements can be easily seen and deciphered.

Letter-spacing - The amount of horizontal space between letters in words; also called tracking in most software programs.

Ligatures - a joining of two or more letters in a word to make the word read better. This can be accomplished by overlapping letters or by actually rendering them as joined.

Linear Perspective - A principle discovered by Filippo Brunelleschi that parallel lines rendered to simulate three-dimensional reality will converge at a single vanishing point.

Logo - A unique symbol for representing the identity of a company; sometimes also called a brand.

Monitor Gamma - The native brightness setting for monitors. For PCs it is set at 0.45; for Macintosh at 0.55 (brighter).

Monogram - A kind of logo that shows the first initial or initials of the company's functional name.

Pixel Mush - When the elements of an image are so fine that there is not even one whole pixel that can show either the object color or the background color but rather some intermediate color.

Prima-Donna - a temperamental person who believes that adulation and deference are his/her due and who does not accept criticism or direction.

Professional - A person who performs duties with competence, always in the client's best interest.

Rectilinear - Formed by or bounded by straight lines.

Reversing - The placing of lighter objects, especially type, over a darker background.

Saturation - The richness or dullness of a color.

Sculpted Type - Words on a curved, non-linear baseline

Self-Brainstorming - a technique for generating concepts with oneself by concentrating on different conceptual approaches and documenting ideas without evaluating them.

Shallow Containment - The act of surrounding a signature with a shape, which adds very little design value.

Signature - The functional name of a company written in a particular font. Generally, these are only suitable for consumer products and the companies that make them and are less suitable for other corporate identities.

Surprinting - The placing of darker objects, especially type, over a lighter background.

Swashes - A curvilinear decorative addition to typography that should not interfere with a word's core letterforms.

Tints - A flat shade in printing produced by a uniform grid of halftone dots, described as percentages of the ink color, with 100% being solid ink, 0% being no ink and the grays in between in accurate percentages of how much paper is covered by the halftone dots.

Tracking - In most software programs the adjustment of the horizontal space between letters in words; also known as letterspacing.

Type Warp - A tool in various graphic computer programs for producing sculpted type. Not recommended due to its inability to treat letters individually but, only as whole words.

Value - The lightness or darkness inherent in any color.

Vanishing - The condition brought about by objects or type and their background being close in both value and hue.

Vector - a kind of graphic computer program that produces infinitely scalable output, as opposed to bitmap or pixel-based imagery.

Vibrating - The condition brought about by objects or type and their background being close in value but very different in hue.

Visual Logic - The way visual elements create expectations in the viewer's mind.

Wannabe - A person who wants to claim achievement without learning the discipline necessary to achieve it.

Wordmark - The company name created with some unique graphic element besides just the font used.

Appendix 2: Logos by A. Michael Shumate

Sparrow Communication
(Advertising Agency)

Confederation
Conference Centre

David Luke Associates
Management Consultants

Expertise Exchange
St. Lawrence College

Eastern P. E. I.
Chamber of Commerce

Xpansion Software*
(Online Vendor)

Tech Value Net
Heyland Medical

CareNet
Heyland Medical

Critical Care Nutrition
Heyland Medical

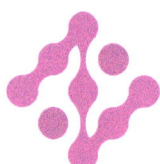

Zap the Vap
Heyland Medical

Clinical Eval Research
Heyland Medical

Latimer Soapworks*

Small Business Assistance
DREE Canada

Nature Illustration

DesignEd Books
Imprint of Boheme Press

Kingston Arts Council

Human Rights Movement
PEI

Millennial Goals
Kingston District: the Church of Jesus Christ of Latter-day Saints

Alexis
Fine Art

Elfstone Press

Explore Economics East
Business Conference

Kane Associates*
Management Consulting

Working Forest PEI
Forest Management

Sustainable Forest
Alliance

Visual Entity
Illustration

Maritime Stone & TImber
Construction

Cargo FX*
Importers

Elementary Science & Technology
Queens University

Island WIde
Hospital Access

Lamb and Lion

WM Services
Property Management

* Unimplemented designs

Index

Also by A. Michael Shumate

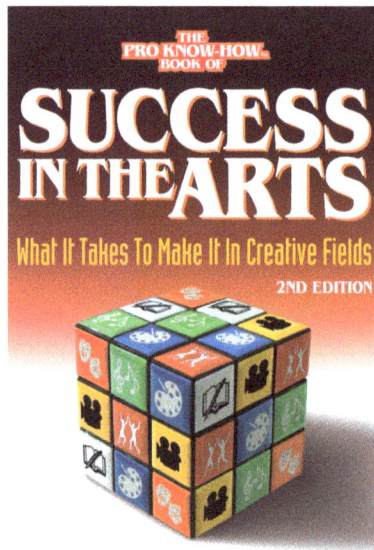

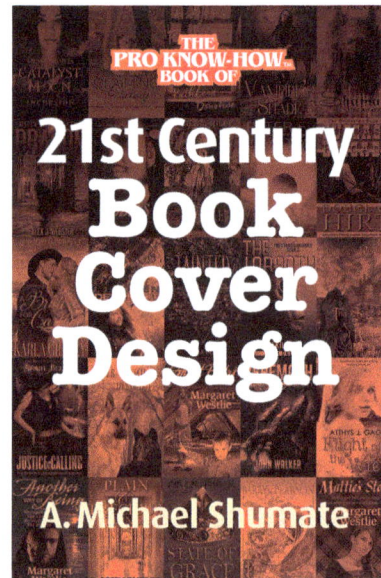

For Artists of All Kinds:
Writers, Musicians, Filmmakers,
Visual Artists, Dancers, Actors

Learn to answer these essential questions:

- What factors contribute most to success in the arts?
- Do you have enough talent?
- What do you need besides talent?
- What are the biggest myths about creativity?
- What is real creativity and how do you cultivate it?
- How do you get through tough times?
- How do you deal with criticism?
- How do you "get the breaks" in your field?
- What foundation principles don't change?
- How do you hang on to the important things in life?
- How do you keep from "selling your soul?"
- What if you don't make it?
- Save years of trial and error.
- Avoid the common pitfalls of creative careers.
- A mentor in a book.

Available wherever books are sold

**Books are not sold
the same way they used to be.**

**That means
book covers can't be designed
the same way they used to be.**

- Learn why book cover design
must be different now

- Discover the
Seven Deadly Sins of Book Cover Design

- Unchanging and immutable principles
for traditional and indie publishers alike

- Design covers that promote more sales

Available wherever books are sold